Pathways to Excellence:
Computing
and ICT

Curriculum for Excellence
CfE

Frank Frame and **John Mason**

DL **DYNAMIC** LEARNING

HODDER GIBSON
AN HACHETTE UK COMPANY

For all the staff and pupils, past and present, that have made Balwearie a great place to work.

The Publishers would like to thank the following for permission to reproduce copyright material:

Photo credits

p.8 (c) © Daniel James Armisha – Fotolia, (bl) © Intel Corporation, (br) © Intel Corporation; p.9 Courtesy of Dell Inc.; p.10 (t) © Vladimir Liverts – Fotolia, (b) © vetkit – Fotolia; p.11 (t) © Sapphire Technology Limited. All rights reserved., (b) © kiselevandrey – Fotolia; p.12 (t) Image reprinted with permission from ViewSonic Corporation, (b) © AFP/Getty Images; p.13 (t) © Greg Pease/Getty Images, (b) © Oxford Events Photography/Alamy; p.14 (t) © Roger Ressmeyer/CORBIS, (bl) © Mozilla Firefox, (bc) © Opera Software ASA, (br) © Google; p.15 (t) © John Kershaw/Alamy, (bl) © Stepan Popov/ iStockphoto.com, (br) © maron – Fotolia; p.17 (both) © 2011 Google; p.19 © Jeff Blackler/ Rex Features; p.22 (t) © BLOOMimage/Getty Images; p.26 © Imagestate Media (John Foxx); p.28 (t) © Tranquil PC Limited Ltd, (c) © Vladimir Liverts – Fotolia, (bl) © Intel Corporation, (br) © maron – Fotolia; p.29 © auris – Fotolia; p.30 (t) © The Carbon Reduction Label is owned by The Carbon Trust Footprinting Company Limited. For further information please visit www.carbon-label.com, (c) © James Steidl – Fotolia, (bl) © Monkey Business – Fotolia, (br) © wrangler – Fotolia; p.31 (t) © The Image Works/TopFoto, (c) © Len Wilcox/Alamy, (b) © THIERRY BERROD, MONA LISA PRODUCTION/ SCIENCE PHOTO LIBRARY; p.32 (t) © Alejandro Mendoza/iStockphoto.com, (cl) [002_14 credit line needed], (cr) © Intel Corporation; p.33 (clockwise from tr) © wrangler – Fotolia, © John Mendoza – Fotolia, © Small Town Studio – Fotolia, © THIERRY BERROD, MONA LISA PRODUCTION/ SCIENCE PHOTO LIBRARY, © The Image Works/TopFoto; p.34 © ADAM HART-DAVIS/SCIENCE PHOTO LIBRARY; p.35 Courtesy of Imperial College London, e-ScienceTalk and GridPP; p.36 Screen shot(s) reprinted with permission from Apple Inc.; p.37 © Monkey Business; p.38 (t) © iofoto/iStockphoto.com, (b) © Skype Limited; p.39 © India Today Group/ Getty Images; p.45 (top row) © Avira Operations GmbH & Co. KG. All rights reserved, (bottom row, l to r) © Kaspersky Lab ZAO, © Norton Internet Security, the 2012 version of the product. Norton is the consumer product from Symantec, © Norton Antivirus, the 2012 version of the product. Norton is the consumer product from Symantec, © G Data Software AG, © Avira Operations GmbH & Co. KG. All rights reserved; p.50 (l to r) © Norton Internet Security, the 2012 version of the product. Norton is the consumer product from Symantec, © Norton Antivirus, the 2012 version of the product. Norton is the consumer product from Symantec, © G Data Software AG; p.95 (t original photo) © John Mason; p.97 (c original photo) © John Mason; p.104 (c original photo) © John Mason, (b original photo) Reproduced with kind permission of Balwearie High School and Fife Council; p.105 (c, bl and br original photos) © John Mason; p.106 (original photo) © John Mason; p.113 (b original photo) © John Mason; p.115 ©2011 Google; p.118 © Mikael Damkier – Fotolia; p.119 (l to r) © Gareth Leung - fotolia.com, © Takako Namiki, © Tony Kyriacou/Rex Features; p.120 © 2011 Twitter; p.121 © 2011 Twitter; p.122 (t) Screen shot(s) reprinted with permission from Apple Inc., (b) ©2011 Google; p.123 Copyright © 2011 members of the Audacity development team. Audacity® is a registered trademark of Dominic Mazzoni; p.125 (t) Facebook © 2011, (b) © 2004 - 2011 Sulake Corporation Oy. HABBO is a registered trademark of Sulake Corporation Oy in the European Union, the USA, Japan, the People's Republic of China and various other jurisdictions. All rights reserved; p.126 (t) Copyright 2006-2011 Muxlim Inc. advisory@muxliminc.com; p.127 (both) Facebook © 2011; p.128 Facebook © 2011; p.129 © Alex Segre/Alamy; p.130 (t) © Getty Images, (cl) with kind permission of Cat Register & Rescue, Scottish Registered Charity SC017796, (cr) The material on page 130 , from http://www.facebook.com/oxfamGB is reproduced with the permission of Oxfam GB, Oxfam House, John Smith Drive, Cowley, Oxford OX4 2JY, UK www.oxfam.org.uk. Oxfam GB does not necessarily endorse any text or activities that accompany the materials, (b) Copyright Guardian News & Media Ltd 2009.

All screenshots in Chapter 4, 'An introduction to programming using Scratch', reproduced with kind permission of Scratch. Scratch is a project of the Lifelong Kindergarten Group at the MIT Media Lab.

All screenshots in Chapter 5, 'Graphics and Animations', reproduced with kind permission of Serif (Europe) Limited. DrawPlus is a registered trademark of Serif (Europe) Limited.

Original photos used in sequence on pages 108–112 inclusive ©2011 Google – Imagery ©2011 TerraMetrics, Map data ©2011 Europa Technologies, GIS Innovatsia, Geocentre Consulting, Google, PPWK, Tele Atlas, Transnavicom.

Every effort has been made to trace all copyright holders, but if any have been inadvertently overlooked the Publishers will be pleased to make the necessary arrangements at the first opportunity.

Although every effort has been made to ensure that website addresses are correct at time of going to press, Hodder Gibson cannot be held responsible for the content of any website mentioned in this book. It is sometimes possible to find a relocated web page by typing in the address of the home page for a website in the URL window of your browser.

Hachette UK's policy is to use papers that are natural, renewable and recyclable products and made from wood grown in sustainable forests. The logging and manufacturing processes are expected to conform to the environmental regulations of the country of origin.

Orders: please contact Bookpoint Ltd, 130 Milton Park, Abingdon, Oxon OX14 4SB; Telephone: (44) 01235 827720; Fax: (44) 01235 400454. Lines are open 9.00–5.00, Monday to Saturday, with a 24-hour message answering service. Visit our website at www.hoddereducation.co.uk. Hodder Gibson can be contacted direct on: Tel: 0141 848 1609; Fax: 0141 889 6315; email: hoddergibson@hodder.co.uk.

© Frank Frame and John Mason 2011
First published in 2011 by
Hodder Gibson, an imprint of Hodder Education,
An Hachette UK Company
2a Christie Street
Paisley PA1 1NB

Impression number   5 4 3 2 1

Year   2014 2013 2012 2011

Cover photo © Dean Mitchell/ iStockphoto

Illustrations by Richard Duszczak and DC Graphic Design Limited, Swanley, Kent

Typeset in DIN light 10pt by DC Graphic Design Limited, Swanley, Kent
Printed in Italy

A catalogue record for this title is available from the British Library.

ISBN: 978 1444 11080 7

Contents

Teacher's introduction

Articulation with senior phase courses

This text has been designed to articulate smoothly between the Curriculum for Excellence level 4 technology outcomes and experiences and the senior phase courses in computing and information science.

The text ensures this articulation by providing opportunities to develop skills and knowledge relevant to software development, computer systems, computer networks, security issues and the wider economic and environmental implications of computing technologies.

It also provides opportunities to develop planning, implementation and evaluation skills which are essential for successful completion of the research-based added-value units in the senior phase courses.

Mapping the content to the outcomes and experiences

The table below clearly shows the relationship between elements of the content of the textbook and a wide range of outcomes and experiences. While the main focus is on computing science and ICT there are plenty of opportunities to address numeracy, literacy and health and wellbeing outcomes and experiences, particularly through the tasks embedded in the text.

Outcome	Topic	Unit
Through research, I can gain knowledge of computer systems or emerging technologies to understand their differing features and consider their suitability for the world of work. TCH 4-08d	Research of emerging technologies	Researching computer technologies
I can debate the possible future impact of new and emerging technologies on economic prosperity and the environment. TCH 4-01c	The economic and environmental impact of new ICT technologies	Computing technology, the economy and the environment →

Outcome	Topic	Unit
I can work with others to plan and use a learning group for sharing experiences, ideas and information within a secure online environment. TCH 4-08a	Using wikis and websites to share ideas and information	Researching computer technologies Computing technology, the economy and the environment Which security suite?
I can compare different forms of security software to gain knowledge and understanding of their functions in protecting contemporary technologies. TCH 4-08b	Security software	Which security suite?
I can integrate different media to create a digital solution which allows interaction and collaboration with others. TCH 4-08c	Creating advanced web pages and blogs	Linking up
By learning the basic principles of a programming language or control technology, I can design a solution to a scenario, implement it and evaluate its success. TCH 4-09a	Advanced use of Scratch	An introduction to programming using Scratch
I can create graphics and animations using appropriate software which utilise my skills and knowledge of the application. TCH 4-09b	Graphics and animations	Graphics and animations
I can use features of software to create my own animation which can then be used to create an animated sequence. TCH 4-09c	Animated sequences	Graphics and animations
Numeracy outcomes		
I can discuss and illustrate the facts I need to consider when determining what I can afford, in order to manage credit and debt and lead a responsible lifestyle. MNU 4-09a	Embedded in tasks	Researching computer technologies Computing technology, the economy and the environment

Outcome	Topic	Unit
Having recognised similarities between new problems and problems I have solved before, I can carry out the necessary calculations to solve problems set in unfamiliar contexts. MNU 4-03a	Embedded in tasks	All units
Using proportion, I can calculate the change in one quantity caused by a change in a related quantity and solve real-life problems. MNU 4-08a	Embedded in tasks	Computing technology, the economy and the environment
I can apply my knowledge and understanding of measure to everyday problems and tasks and appreciate the practical importance of accuracy when making calculations. MNU 4-11a	Embedded in tasks	Computing technology, the economy and the environment
Literacy outcomes		
I can independently select ideas and relevant information for different purposes, organise essential information or ideas and any supporting detail in a logical order, and use suitable vocabulary to communicate effectively with my audience. LIT 3-06a/4-06a	Opportunities embedded in group work tasks	All units
When listening and talking with others for different purposes, I can: ■ communicate detailed information, ideas or opinions ■ explain processes, concepts or ideas with some relevant supporting detail ■ sum up ideas, issues, findings or conclusions. LIT 4-09a	Opportunities embedded in group work tasks	All units
Using what I know about the features of different types of texts, I can find, select, sort, summarise, link and use information from different sources. LIT 3-14a/LIT 4-14a	Opportunities embedded in tasks	All units
I can make notes and organise them to develop my thinking, help retain and recall information, explore issues and create new texts, using my own words as appropriate. LIT 3-15a/LIT 4-15a	Opportunities embedded in tasks	All units

→

Outcome	Topic	Unit
I can use a range of strategies and resources independently and ensure that my spelling, including specialist vocabulary, is accurate. LIT 4-21a	Opportunities embedded in tasks	All units
Throughout the writing process, I can review and edit my writing independently to ensure that it meets its purpose and communicates meaning clearly at the first reading. LIT 4-23a	Opportunities embedded in tasks	All units
I can consider the impact that layout and presentation will have on my reader, selecting and using a variety of features appropriate to purpose and audience. LIT 4-24a	Opportunities embedded in tasks	All units
I can use notes and other types of writing to generate and develop ideas, retain and recall information, explore problems, make decisions, or create original text. I can make appropriate and responsible use of sources and acknowledge these appropriately. LIT 4-25a	Opportunities embedded in tasks	All units
I can convey information and describe events, explain processes or concepts, providing substantiating evidence, and synthesise ideas or opinions in different ways. LIT 4-28a	Opportunities embedded in tasks	All units
I can persuade, argue, evaluate, explore issues or express and justify opinions within a convincing line of thought, using relevant supporting detail and/or evidence. LIT 4-29a	Opportunities embedded in tasks	All units
Health and wellbeing outcomes		
I am developing the skills to lead and recognise strengths of group members, including myself. I contribute to groups and teams through my knowledge of individual strengths, group tactics and strategies. HWB 4-23a	Opportunities embedded in group work tasks	All units
I am learning to assess and manage risk, to protect myself and others, and to reduce the potential for harm when possible. HWB 0-16a/HWB 1-16a/HWB 2-16a/HWB 3-16a/HWB 4-16a	Opportunities embedded in text and tasks	Which security suite?

Cross-curricular projects

These will naturally follow from interaction with classes and colleagues in other areas of the curriculum.

Some flow naturally from the topics relevant to computing science and ICT outcomes. For example, a joint project with the science department on greenhouse gases would be very relevant when investigating the environmental impact of the use of computer technology.

Assessment

There are many opportunities for the teacher to adopt techniques based on 'Assessment is For Learning' (see below) and to monitor and support progress at each stage of the learning process.

Learners are also encouraged to monitor and evaluate their own progress, as well as reflect on what and how they have learned, by completing self-assessment questionnaires which are to be found in the Appendix at the back of the book, and electronic versions are available in Pathways to Excellence: Computing and ICT Dynamic Learning. Visit **www.dynamic-learning.co.uk** for more information.

Pedagogy

Active learning

The use of active learning approaches to learning and teaching is a key component of the delivery of computing science and ICT outcomes and experiences as its main focus is on helping learners engage with the curriculum.

Key points of active learning

Sharing outcomes

Sharing outcomes/success criteria at the start of a lesson in order to identify ways of demonstrating learning and monitoring progress.

Linking to existing knowledge

Drawing out and working with existing knowledge and skills which pupils bring to the classroom and moving from the familiar to the unfamiliar particularly when developing problem-solving skills.

Using small steps

Tackling difficult concepts in small steps to then elaborate, enhance and exemplify.

Employing a structured use of discussion

- Focusing on key learning outcomes.
- Incorporating the use of skilled questioning techniques including opportunities to respond to 'open' questions.
- Giving time to think and reflect.
- Making progressive cognitive demands during questioning including progression of problem-solving contexts.
- Valuing individual responses.

Flexible grouping

Employing flexible grouping strategies: engaging with individuals and small groups within a class.

Demonstrating understanding

Giving learners the opportunity to demonstrate their understanding in a variety of ways by explaining information, ideas and processes to their teacher and other learners in their own words using the presentations websites, wikis or posters which they have produced either individually or as part of a group.

Such learner-led demonstrations and presentations can become the focus of class discussion on the merits and achievements of individuals and groups and help formulate criteria for further peer- and self-assessment.

Group work

Opportunities for group work are embedded throughout the units. Group work is encouraged because learners can develop their understanding and learning skills through working with other people. Also, cooperative learning helps young people develop the interpersonal skills and attitudes which are highly regarded both in the world of work and in a range of social contexts.

A key element of successful group work is building group skills, such as listening, discussing, organising and giving positive feedback.

A set of guidelines designed to support effective group work is in Unit 1 on pages 23–25.

Assessment is for Learning

The approach to assessment which fits ideally with active learning is 'Assessment is for Learning' (AIFL).

Key aspects of AIFL

- Changing the balance between formative and summative assessment, placing more emphasis on formative assessment.
- Using assessment to support the next stages of learning by adapting teaching and learning activities.
- Viewing assessment as designed to highlight learners' strengths and weaknesses and directing learners' steps to improvement.
- Sharing learning intentions/success criteria so that learners know when they have been successful.
- Giving and receiving supportive feedback builds confidence and encourages improvement.
- Using peer- and self-assessment to enable learners to develop the skills necessary to evaluate their own and others' work.
- Providing opportunities for learners to reflect and analyse their own learning and make adjustments.

The key outcome of AIFL is that children know their own strengths and needs, and are clear and confident about what is needed to improve.

There are opportunities throughout the text to employ this approach to assessment, and questionnaires which can be used to stimulate reflective self-assessment are in the Appendix at the back of the book.

1

Researching computer technologies

In this unit you are going to find out about computer systems and new technologies by completing a series of research projects. However, before you start your research you need to understand some important computing terms and we shall explore these below.

The portfolio

As you work through the first three chapters of this book, you are going to build up a portfolio which will hold all the documents you produce for each of the projects and tasks.

Before you begin you should set up a folder called *Portfolio* and use it to store all the documents you produce as you work through each chapter. Your portfolio should have subfolders for each project or research task you complete named, for example, Unit1research1 or Unit2project1 etc.

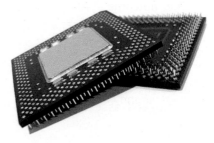

Important computing terminology

The processor

The processor is the 'brain' of the computer that deals with all the movement of data and any calculations to be carried out. A processor is made of silicon crystal wafers which hold millions of tiny electronic components

You will find that modern computer systems have two or more processors working together to make the system work better. You will find systems with duo-processors, with two processors working together, and quad processors, with four processors working together, and even a hexa-core processor with six processors.

Clock speed

Clock speeds are a measure of how powerful a processor is. The clock pulses, measured in GHz, regulate and co-ordinate the activities in the processor. Processor clock speeds are changing all the time.

> 1 Gigahertz (GHz) = 1000 million pulses per second.
>
> 1 Megahertz (MHz) = 1 million pulses per second.

Research task

■ Use the Internet to find out the speeds of the latest processors.

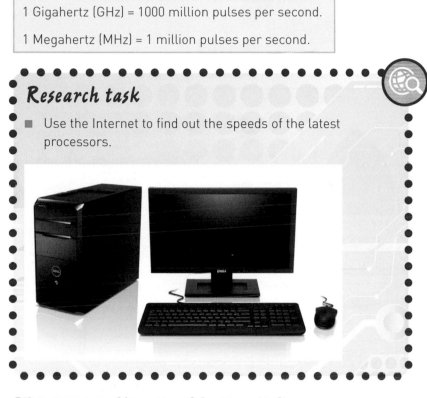

Other measures of how powerful a computer is

There are other measures of how powerful a computer system is, for example, the size of the internal RAM memory, the size of the backing storage such as the hard drive, and how good the graphics card and sound card are.

Computer memory

The **main memory** can be either **RAM** or **ROM**. ROM (**R**ead **O**nly **M**emory) is system memory, it holds vital systems information like startup instructions.

RAM (**R**andom **A**ccess **M**emory) is the working space of the computer. It holds all the programs and data files currently in use by the system and the user.

Key points about RAM

- The processor can write to, or read from, RAM at high speed.
- Data held in RAM can be changed.
- All data in RAM is **lost** when the power is switched off.
- Holds all the data and programs currently in use.

Key points about ROM

- Data are stored permanently in ROM, it is **not lost** when the power goes off.
- Data in the ROM cannot be changed.
- Holds vital systems data and programs.

Measuring the size of memory

We use these terms to measure the computer's memory.

Bit	Binary digit: a single 1 or 0
Byte	8 Bits e.g. 11001110
Kilobyte	1024 Bytes
Megabyte	1024 Kilobytes
Gigabyte	1024 Megabytes
Terabyte	1024 Gigabytes

Graphics cards

These cards contain a processor and memory and are plugged directly into your computer's motherboard. They are specialised pieces of hardware to process sound or graphics images, freeing up the main processor so that it can get on with other tasks. A good graphics card can speed up gameplay on a PC, as the main processor no longer needs to work out what the screen should look like and display it. Graphics cards are constantly getting more powerful.

If you are researching a system which has a graphics card you need to use your search engines to check the Internet for the latest information on the graphics cards processors and RAM.

Research task

- Search the Internet for two graphics cards, compare them according to their processor speed and RAM capacity and then choose one giving your reasons. Your teacher will set you a budget for your purchase.
- Below is an example of a comparison to guide you.

Graphics card	Graphics processor speed	RAM capacity
The NVIDIA GeForce 9800 GTX	675 MHz	512 Megabytes
Sapphire Radeon HD 4850 X2	625 MHz	2 Gigabytes

Choice

I would choose the Sapphire Radeon because it has a larger memory size. Memory is very important when dealing with graphics and I think it's better to have the Sapphire with 2 Gigabytes than the NVIDIA even though it has a slightly faster clock speed.

Sound cards

Computer systems use sound cards to capture audio data. Sound cards do this by taking tens of thousands of samples of analogue sound waves each second. They then change each sample into a binary number and store each sample in memory.

This can make very heavy demands on the processor and memory. For example, if a sound is sampled at 44 KHz, the processor has to convert 44000 analogue quantities to binary form every second and then store each one.

Sound cards have their own on-board processors and memory units to take the strain off the computer's own processor and main memory. Without a sound card the system would slow down.

Screen resolution

This determines the quality of images that can be displayed, e.g. a 1680 x 1050 high resolution screen or a 1280 x 1024 medium resolution.

Screen with a 1440×900 resolution

Research task

- Search the Internet for two sound cards and compare them according to their processor speed and RAM capacity then choose one giving your reasons.
- Your teacher will set you a budget for your purchase.

Research task

- You have to purchase a new TFT (thin film transistor) screen. Your teacher will set you a budget for your purchase.
- Search the Internet for two TFT screens and compare them according to their resolution, then choose one giving your reasons.

Simulation

Simulations can be used to train people and to help them develop skills, such as driving a car or flying a plane, by using a computer-based model.

Simulators can be very realistic and accurate ways of training people to handle complex machinery in an environment where a learner's mistakes are not dangerous or costly.

Researching computer technologies

Using flight simulation, a trainee pilot can experience many different types of emergency without any risk to people or expensive equipment.

Research task

■ Search the Internet for an example of the use of simulation for training. Produce a report in the form of a presentation. Your report should include key points of information and relevant graphics and hyperlinks to useful websites.

Simulation can also be used for leisure, for example, simulation computer games and simulated rides in theme parks.

Virtual reality

A virtual reality (VR) system is an advanced form of simulation that can create the illusion that the user is part of the computer's world and can move about and manipulate that world.

Virtual reality systems can be used for:

■ training people to drive a car, fly a plane or run a nuclear reactor.
■ creating a 3-D plan of a new construction which can be looked at from all angles – even from the inside! A plan of a building or even a whole town can be simulated using a VR system.
■ for games and leisure activities – the sky is no limit in VR!

A range of specialised sensors that detect movement are fitted to the gloves, suits and headsets worn by the user. The user can point to, lift and 'touch' objects in the virtual world. The headset has a pair of small screens that create a 3-D visual effect. The feeling of reality is improved by sound from headphones to immerse the user in the world of the computer.

Research task

■ Search the Internet for an example of the use of VR for games and entertainment. Produce a report in the form of a presentation. Your report should include key points of information and relevant graphics and hyperlinks to useful websites. This website should help you:
http://www.amusitronix.com/

Browser

A **browser** is a program that helps you navigate the **World Wide Web**, move between and look at web pages by entering the address of the page you want or clicking on a hyperlink. Examples of browsers are Internet Explorer®, Firefox®, Opera™ and Google Chrome™.

Google Chrome

Search engine

Search engines are used to look for web pages. A simple search has one item or topic in the search e.g. 'computer network LAN'.

The search engine will find all the web pages related to that topic and send the results to your computer for your browser to display them. Examples of search engines are Google™ search, Yahoo!®, Blackle™ and AltaVista®.

Server

A **server** is a powerful computer with a fast processor and large memory capacity. A server provides the **resources** on a network.

A network can have a range of servers such as:

- **print** server, controlling printing resources
- **file** server, controlling access to files
- **application** server, controlling access to application packages
- **mail** server, storing and passing email
- **web** server, controlling access to the Internet.

Systems analyst

A systems analyst designs new systems or improves existing ones. Systems analysis involves finding out which tasks the system has to carry out and then deciding on the computer system and software needed.

Backing storage

The backing storage is the part of the computer system where the data are stored: the hard drives, DVDs, CDs or USB flash drives.

Complete this table using the words in the box below

	This processes the images on your computer, freeing up the main processor so that it can get on with other tasks.
	This person's task is to decide what hardware and software is needed.
	This is used to describe the quality of an image on a screen, e.g. 1280 x 1024.
	This is a program that helps you navigate the World Wide Web by moving between and looking at web pages.
	This is a powerful computer with a fast processor and large memory capacity which provides the resources on a network, e.g. file storage.
	This processes the sounds on your computer, freeing up the main processor so that it can get on with other tasks.
	The 'brain' of the computer that deals with all the movement of data and any calculations to be carried out.
	This part of memory holds all of the programs and data files currently in use by the system and the user.
	This uses computer-based models to train people and to help them develop skills, such as driving a car or flying a plane.
	This is used to measure the size of memory and hard drive capacity.
	This is used to measure the clock speed of a processor.
	This is an advanced form of simulation that can create the illusion that the user is part of the computer's world.

browser   systems analyst   virtual reality   sound card   simulation   RAM   processor   GHz
graphics card   resolution   Gigabyte   server

Your research-based project

Your research-based project will have several stages: choosing the topic, searching for information, organising your information and producing a report.

Choosing the topic

There is a wide range of topics for you to choose from. You can choose any computer system, e.g. the latest laptop, gaming machine or smartphone. You could choose a service on the Internet, e.g. e-commerce: the use of the Internet to buy and sell goods and investigate sites like eBay or Amazon. You could research the use of video conferencing or cloud computing. You could even research a new piece of computing technology that has just come on the market such as an e-reader, the iPad® 2, in-car computer systems, fold-up keyboards, biochips and biosensors or virtual reality.

If you are working as part of a group you should discuss your choice of topic in the group as well as with your teacher.

Searching for information

There are two main sources of information that you could use: computer magazines and the Internet. Your teacher may have a series of magazine articles which you can look through to help you find information. These can be very useful especially when it comes to looking for the latest developments since magazines like *PCPro* and *PCAdviser* review the latest technologies that come onto the market. You can even check out these magazines online.

You will also use search engines like Google™ search, Yahoo! and Ask Jeeves™ to find information.

Using a search engine

You can find that using a search engine can get you too much information and return hundreds of thousands of web pages. It would take you far too long to search through all the pages that your search turns up.

The trick is to narrow your search down by making it more precise.

You can do this in two ways: first, by making sure that your search contains as much information as possible, e.g. rather than searching for 'laptops' search for 'laptops with 4 Gigabytes of RAM memory and a TFT display'. The simple search for laptops found over 74,000,000 webpages, far too many!

About 74,900,000 results (0.15 seconds)

Second, you can use your search engine's advanced search facility which helps you narrow down the range of your search and make it more precise.

Organising your information

When you have finished searching for information you will have a collection of useful web pages and/or magazine articles.

You must not make the mistake of thinking that all you have to do next is copy and paste large chunks of information in order to make up your report!

Choose the key points

You have to read each page or article carefully and choose the key points to use in your report. You will need to practise this as it is a key skill!

Read this article about docking stations. The key points have been highlighted for you.

A docking station is a bridge to the past for many newer computers, but you might find you need one even if you have the latest on-the-market laptop computer. A docking station is a device into which you can plug your laptop in order to gain extra functionality, such as access to printers, mice, scanners, full-sized monitors and keyboards, and external hard drives. All of these peripherals can be plugged into the docking station. Then, when you connect the laptop to the docking station, you can gain access to all of those peripherals without having to plug each one into the laptop. This can be especially helpful if your laptop has a minimal number of USB or Firewire ports.

In essence, using a docking station converts your laptop computer into a desktop computer, whenever it suits you. You can plug the laptop into the docking station and have all the comforts of home, while accessing the laptop's data and functionality. When you're done, just unplug and walk away with the laptop. In some cases, the laptop, which is likely a newer computer than the desktop, will have more up-to-date or advanced features. For example, the laptop may have a super-charged graphics or video card that can play games or movies that the desktop cannot; hooking the laptop up to the docking station and accessing the desktop's larger monitor can make the video or gaming experience all the more rewarding.

The next step is to gather the key points together. In our example the key points have been gathered together for you:

- 'a docking station is a device into which you can plug your laptop to gain access to printers, mice, scanners, full-sized monitors and keyboards, and external hard drives'
- 'a docking station converts your laptop computer into a desktop computer, whenever it suits you'
- 'the laptop may have a super-charged graphics or video card that can play games or movies that the desktop cannot'
- 'accessing the desktop's larger monitor'.

Combining the key points

Finally you need to combine the key points into a short paragraph which gives clear information about your topic **using your own words**. The key points about docking stations have been combined below:

> A docking station is a device you can use to connect your laptop to printers, mice, scanners, full-sized monitors, keyboards, and external hard drives. It lets you use your laptop computer like a desktop computer whenever you want so that you could use your laptop's graphics or video card and your desktop's large monitor to play games or watch movies.

Key points task

Produce a short paragraph after reading the following article on e-book reader displays. The key points have been highlighted for you.

The e-book reader display

One complaint some people had about early e-book readers was that it can be difficult to read words on an LCD display. Some users complained that longer reading sessions put too much strain on their eyes. Amazon's solution was to use electronic ink technology. The Kindle's electronic ink screen looks more like paper than an LCD screen. It reflects light in much the same way that paper does. The screen lacks a backlight, so you'll need daylight or an external light source such as a lamp in order to read anything.

Why would you want to use an e-book reader in the first place? One reason is that an e-book reader can hold many titles. The Amazon Kindle 2 can hold up to 1500 titles (books, newspapers, magazines and blogs) in its memory. The original Kindle also had a port that allowed users to save titles to a memory card, extending the device's capacity. Some people like the idea of having an electronic library that takes up very little physical space.

The Kindle's memory capacity also makes it very convenient for travellers. With a Kindle, you don't have to worry about packing heavy books in your luggage to last for the whole trip. A single Kindle can hold more than enough titles to tide you over. And if you decide you want something completely different midway through the trip (as long as you're travelling in a country in which Amazon offers service for its international Kindle), you can always use the Kindle to access Amazon's store and buy a new book.

Article extract from 'How the Amazon Kindle Works' by Jonathan Strickland, available online at **http://electronics.howstuffworks.com/gadgets/travel/amazon-kindle.htm**

Key points task

Produce a short paragraph after reading the following article on 'cloud computing'.
You will have to decide what the key points are, then combine them.

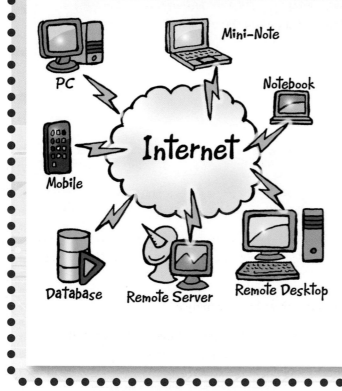

Cloud computing customers do not own the hardware that provides their computing power and storage, instead they rent shared access to their computers from a *cloud company*.

The customers pay only for what they use and pay the bill every month or every three months, in the same way as they pay for their electricity.

This helps reduce the costs involved since businesses can avoid spending lots of money on hardware and software.

It's also very flexible since the businesses can increase or decrease the number of computers, the number and type of software as it suits them.

Producing a research report

Your research report should be structured as follows:

- A short description of the system/new technology which contains a list of the key features of the system/new technology.
- A description of each of the features.
- A description of the implications of the use of the system. This will vary according to the system you have chosen but could include your thoughts on ways in which it could make people's working lives better or more efficient, how it could affect the environment, security, any implications for training, finance and the economy.

Here is a report that has been completed on 'cloud computing'. This should act as a guide to help you complete your own report. Note this has been produced after further research based on the article at the top of the page.

Report on cloud computing

What is 'cloud computing'?

'Cloud computing' is the use of the Internet to provide computing services. Instead of a business setting up and owning their own powerful computer systems and network, they buy simple devices that enable them to access the Internet and then use the software, backing storage and servers provided by the cloud computing providers.

Key features of cloud computing

Cloud computing customers:

■ do not own the physical infrastructure.

The powerful servers which provide the computing power are owned by the cloud computing provider.

■ can rent storage space on servers.

Customers can have a contract which enables them to decide how much storage space they need for their data. This arrangement can be very flexible and customers can easily scale their storage up or down as required.

■ can have access to powerful networks without a great initial expense.

A business does not need to spend large amounts of money buying and installing expensive computer systems and networks in order to access powerful computing resources.

■ can access a wide range of application software and software for developing applications.

As soon as the contract is signed a customer can have instant access to all the software, e.g. databases, accounting software, programming software, it needs without having to buy the hardware or pay for and install the software.

■ have access to technical support.

Technical support is supplied by the cloud provider as a standard part of their service.

■ are billed for their service based either on the time they spend using the network or on a monthly or quarterly basis.

Payment can be very flexible. A business that only needs to use the cloud services for short periods of time will be billed according to the hours and minutes spent online. Others will be billed on a regular monthly/quarterly basis.

Some customers have what is called a 'hybrid cloud system' where important data is stored locally. Security concerns mean that some customers keep what is called 'mission critical data' in computer storage devices in their offices.

➡️

Implications of the use of cloud computing for the world of work

Costs and savings

In cloud computing, customers can save a lot of money on their computing costs because they:

- Do not need to pay for a systems analyst and expensive installation and maintenance.
- Do not need to buy hardware and software; they only need a simple system and browser software.
- Do not need to pay for technical support.
- Only need to pay for what they use and can even be charged by the hour or the minute if that suits their needs.

Efficiency

Cloud computing increases the efficient use of computer systems. A business which sets up and maintains its own computer network might find that its systems are only being used fully part of the time. With cloud computing, a business needs only to access computing resources when they are needed. This reduces not only costs but also energy use, an important environmental factor!

Flexibility

Cloud computing is a very flexible way for a business to use computing services. A business can scale up or down the use of backing storage, increase its demands on processing power or adapt the range of software it uses easily, simply by contacting its cloud provider.

Environmental issues

The use of cloud computing by businesses means that there is less need for complex systems since the powerful servers that businesses need to use are provided centrally.

This will reduce the need for businesses to constantly update hardware which, in turn, will reduce the need to recycle old, potentially polluting, computer systems.

Security

Cloud providers do have good security systems in place to protect data but some businesses and organisations are reluctant to have all their data stored on cloud servers. They keep sensitive data, sometimes called 'mission critical data' on servers which they own and control, held locally in their offices. This is known as a 'hybrid' system since it combines cloud computing with their own computing systems.

Note

This report could be produced as a word-processed document, a presentation slide show, web pages or a wiki. An example of this report as a website is available as part of the Dynamic Learning resources. See **www.dynamic-learning.co.uk** for more details.

Choose your research topic

Now you have to decide on a topic for your research and report. You can choose any topic from the list below or you can choose a computing-based topic that you are interested in:

- the latest laptop, gaming machine or smartphone
- video conferencing
- cloud computing
- e-reader
- the iPad® 2
- in-car computer systems
- fold-up keyboards
- biochips and biosensors
- virtual reality.

Your teacher will help you make your choice. You can also research and report on any of the latest computing-based technologies that you have recently read about in computing magazines or on the web. Good websites to keep you in touch with latest technologies are:

- **http://www.engadget.com/**
- **http://www.gadgetfind.com/**
- **http://www.latest-gadgets.info/**
- **http://news.cnet.com/**

Working as a group

You may decide to research your project and produce your report as part of a group.

Advice on how to tackle the group project

Form your group, ideally of three or four. Your teacher will help you form your group if need be. Once your teacher has helped you decide on a topic for your project you need to follow these steps.

Researching computer technologies

1 Draw up a plan in which you decide how to tackle the project

Draw up your plan using the group project planning sheet in the Appendix on page 144 and involve *all* members of your group in the discussion. You should each explain your ideas and listen carefully to the ideas of the other members. There is an example group planning sheet on pages 48–49 in Unit 3.

Your plan should:

- Map out the task that each person in the group is being given. Each person could have a different role to play, e.g. someone to research for information or graphics, someone to record the information and someone to set up the wiki or e-group. Or each person could research and record the information on the topic and then the group could work together to assemble the wiki or upload the files to the e-group.
- Explain how you are going to get your information. This may be from magazine articles which your teacher provides and/or using search engines to find information on the Internet.
- Describe how you are going to record your information. In the beginning you should store your information as word processing files. This is because you will need to work together as a group and discuss your findings and decide what to put into your final wiki.
- Explain how you are going to communicate with your group members: as well as face-to-face meetings you could use email or an e-group to share and swap data and ideas.
- Describe how you are going to present your information. Your choice for this project is to produce a wiki, a presentation or a website.
- Show how you are going to manage the time your teacher gives you for the project. This will mean setting out deadlines, lesson by lesson, which you should aim to keep to.

2 Stick to the ground rules

You must remember that there are ground rules for group behaviour.

- Take part in group discussions, don't just sit and listen to other people's ideas.
- When discussing ideas be constructive and if you are not happy with a suggestion then criticise the idea and not the person making it.
- Respond to emails from group members promptly.
- Meet your deadlines set out in the planning document. Remember other people in the group are depending on you.

3 Start the research

Once you have completed your group project planning sheet it is time to begin the research.

4 Produce the report

There is an example report on pages 50–51 in Unit 3.

5 Carry out a self-assessment

You will be asked to assess your own individual contribution to the group task by filling in a progress checklist and a questionnaire. Also, you will be asked to fill in a questionnaire to assess the work of the group as a whole. Self-assessment checklists can be found in the Appendix at the back of the book.

6 Produce materials which your teacher will use for assessment

Your teacher will ask you to place the working files you used to store the information you collected from magazines and the Internet in your portfolio.

If your teacher has access to the dynamic learning materials you will be asked to complete some online quizzes.

Your teacher will also assess the group's wiki or e-group when you have completed the project as well as how well you have worked as a group.

Computing technology, the economy and the environment

2

The importance of computing technology

Computing technology is very important. It is used in all our organisations and businesses. We rely on computers to run all our businesses and organisations efficiently.

Progress check!

Using your word processor, copy and complete this list of the places where you will find computing technology at work:

schools, hospitals, doctor's surgery, factories, libraries

Save the document as 'Unit2Task1' and store it in your portfolio.

Using energy

Our computers use up lots of energy. A quick calculation will make it clear!

A desktop computer uses 140 watts per hour and the LCD screen uses 35 watts per hour and the electricity costs 10p per kilowatt hour.

The energy used by the whole system, if it is left powered up all day is 175 x 24 kilowatt hours = 4176 watt hours per day = 4.176 kilowatt hours.

In one year that = 365 x 4.176 kilowatt hours = 1486.65 kilowatt hours. That is a lot of electricity.

It is also expensive. At a cost of 10p per kilowatt hour, the total cost = £148. 65

Using energy can add to the amount of greenhouse gases that we release into the atmosphere, so, running our computers does add to global warming!

Calculate the yearly cost of running a desktop computer which is energy efficient and uses 50 watts per hour with the cost being 10p per kilowatt hour.

Use a spread sheet to calculate the cost then save the document as 'Unit2Task2' and store it in your portfolio.

Project 1

Research and report on four of the latest low-power PCs.

Make sure you follow this step-by-step guide:

- Complete a group project planning sheet (see the Appendix on page 144).
- Include a description of the computer and clearly mention the amount of power it uses expressed in watts per hour.
- Produce your report in the form of a slide presentation, a web page or a wiki.
- Include graphics and a calculation of the cost to run each PC 24 hours a day seven days a week for a year, based on the cost of 10p per kilowatt hour. It should also make clear the advantages of using low-power PCs to businesses and the environment.
- Complete individual checklists and questionnaires and a group questionnaire, copies of which you will find in the Appendix.
- Add the following documents to the 'unit2project1' folder in your portfolio: planning sheets, copies of your checklist and questionnaires as well as your presentation or hyperlinks to your wiki or website.

As a guide here is a report on one low-power PC.

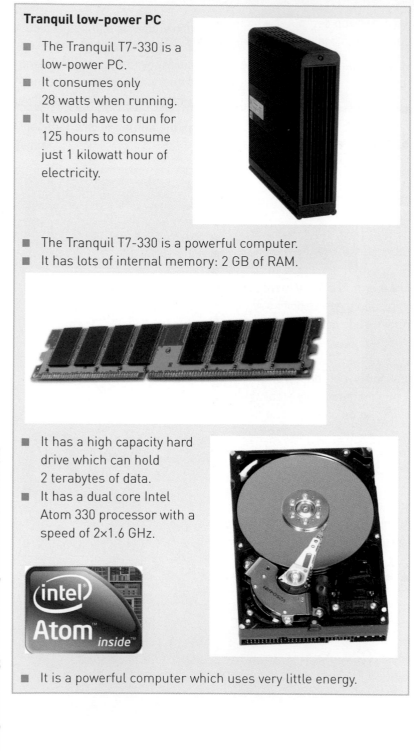

Tranquil low-power PC

- The Tranquil T7-330 is a low-power PC.
- It consumes only 28 watts when running.
- It would have to run for 125 hours to consume just 1 kilowatt hour of electricity.

- The Tranquil T7-330 is a powerful computer.
- It has lots of internal memory: 2 GB of RAM.

- It has a high capacity hard drive which can hold 2 terabytes of data.
- It has a dual core Intel Atom 330 processor with a speed of 2×1.6 GHz.

- It is a powerful computer which uses very little energy.

Project 2

A number of manufacturers, notably Samsung, are producing very low-power monitors which consume around 6 watts. The average LCD monitor consumes around 23 watts!

Research and report on four of the latest low-power monitors.

Make sure you follow this step-by-step guide:

- Complete a group project planning sheet (see the Appendix on page 144).
- Include a description of the computer and clearly mention the amount of power it uses expressed in watts per hour.
- Produce your report in the form of a slide presentation, a web page or a wiki.
- Include graphics and a calculation of the cost to run each monitor 24 hours a day seven days a week for a year, based on the cost of 10p per kilowatt hour. It should also make clear the advantages of using low-power PCs to businesses and the environment.
- Complete individual checklists and questionnaires and a group questionnaire, copies of which you will find in the Appendix.
- Add the following documents to the 'unit2project2' folder in your portfolio: planning sheets, copies of your checklist and questionnaires as well as your presentation or hyperlinks to your wiki or website.

Carbon footprint

When you research new technology, you should not only look at how it will be used and how it will make businesses and organisations run more efficiently, you should also look at its carbon footprint.

The carbon footprint is a measure of the impact that the manufacture and use of computers has on the environment by calculating the amount of greenhouse gases produced.

There are two sides to the question of the carbon footprint of computers.

reducing with
the Carbon Trust

CO2

We have committed to
reduce the carbon footprint
of this product

carbon-label.com

The negative side

On the **negative side** computers do add to the amount of greenhouse gases produced. Computer systems contribute about two per cent of global greenhouse gas emissions, nearly the same amount as the airline industry.

The desktops and laptops we use at home use lots of energy, as you have seen. But so too do the servers and equipment needed to keep the Internet running.

One estimate is that a minute spent on the Internet causes 1.2 grams of carbon dioxide to be emitted into the environment. This is the same as driving a kilometre in a modern, fuel-efficient car.

The positive side

On the **positive side**, the use of computer technology can help decrease the carbon footprint of businesses and organisations by increasing their efficiency and reducing the demand for air travel, and electricity. Some examples are:

■ reducing fuel consumption by using on-board computers to make cars run more efficiently.

■ attaching smart meters and sensors to networks and using them to turn off electrical appliances and adjust lighting to save energy.

■ using computer systems to design and produce a whole range of products that use less energy and fewer natural resources.

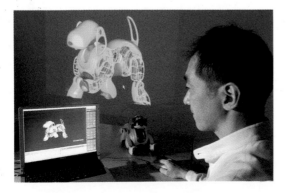

Servers

Servers are powerful computers that:

- store the information on the Internet
- help us communicate across the Internet
- send our emails and search for web pages for us.

They use lots of energy and this produces lots of CO_2.

All of the companies that make and run servers are now designing and using servers that are smaller and more energy efficient so that they will emit less carbon and cost less.

Low-power processors

The companies that make processors that power our computers are designing new low-power processors to save energy.

These processors power the devices we use such as laptops, netbooks and smartphones for our business and personal uses, making them run efficiently and save energy.

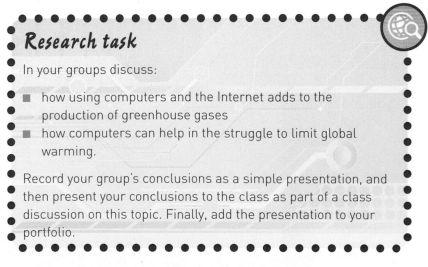

Research task

In your groups discuss:

- how using computers and the Internet adds to the production of greenhouse gases
- how computers can help in the struggle to limit global warming.

Record your group's conclusions as a simple presentation, and then present your conclusions to the class as part of a class discussion on this topic. Finally, add the presentation to your portfolio.

Here is a partially completed record of a group discussion on this topic.

Computers and greenhouse gases

- Using a computer uses energy.
- This releases CO_2 into the atmosphere.
- Just like driving a car.
- Computers can make cars more efficient.
- More efficient servers can reduce the energy that computers use when on the Internet.

- We can use computer systems to design and produce a whole range of products that use less energy and fewer natural resources.

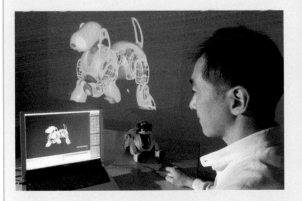

The challenge for new computing technologies

New computing technologies face a challenge to be both more efficient and help people at work and at leisure as well as to be more kind to the environment.

If we are more creative and imaginative in the way we use computing technology we can be more efficient and take care of the environment.

Three examples of creative and imaginative approaches are cloud computing, grid computing and downloading music.

Cloud computing

Cloud computing businesses and organisations do not own the powerful computers that process and store their data. Instead they buy cheap systems that allow them to access the Internet and then rent computing power and storage space from cloud computing providers.

This is very green because it means that less resources are needed to produce computers and less energy is used running them. In effect, they are sharing powerful computers with other users rather than buying, maintaining and running their own!

Grid computing

In grid computing, large numbers of computers connected by a network work together to solve complex problems such as medical research, analysing the forces that produce earthquakes or the Search for Extra-Terrestrial Intelligence (SETI).

The SETI project is designed so that anyone using the Internet can donate some of their computing power to help analyse the data found in the search for radio signals or other forms of communication in space, in an effort to prove the existence of extra-terrestrial intelligence.

Another famous use of grid computing is the Large Hadron Collider at CERN which is used for research into physics.

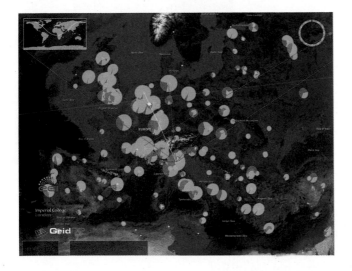

Project 3

Produce a group report on cloud computing and grid computing.

As well as reading the information above on cloud and grid computing you should search the Internet for more data.

Make sure you follow this step-by-step guide:

- Complete a group project planning sheet (see the Appendix on page 144).
- Include a description of cloud and grid computing.
- Produce your report in the form of a slide presentation, a web page or a wiki.
- Include graphics and links to useful websites and possibly video/sound clips.
- Make clear the advantages of using cloud and grid computing to businesses and the environment.
- Complete individual checklists and questionnaires and a group questionnaire, copies of which you will find in the Appendix.
- Add the following documents to the 'unit3project3' folder in your portfolio: planning sheets, copies of your checklist and questionnaires as well as your presentation or hyperlinks to your wiki or website.

Downloading music

Did you know that by downloading music you reduce greenhouse gases by up to 80 per cent for each CD? If you download a series of tracks then burn it onto a CD, then you reduce greenhouse gases by 40 per cent. However, if you download your CD and just store it on your hard drive then the reduction rises to 80 per cent!

This is because using the Internet to download the music tracks saves in the production, burning, transport and delivery of CDs. Not only that, you don't need to spend time or energy getting to and from a music store! This is an example of the use of computers and the Internet saving energy and resources. For the music companies it lowers the cost of producing and distributing CDs and so makes their business more efficient.

This graph shows the number of grams of CO_2 produced in the production and distribution of a music CD.

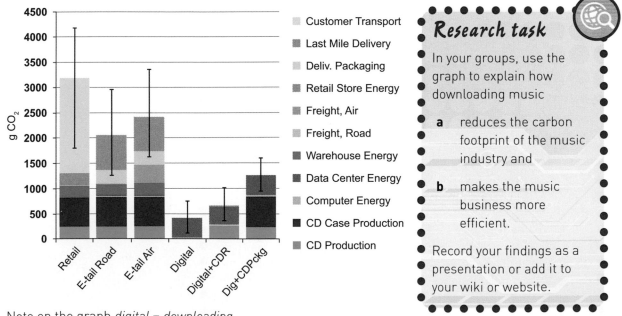

Legend:
- Customer Transport
- Last Mile Delivery
- Deliv. Packaging
- Retail Store Energy
- Freight, Air
- Freight, Road
- Warehouse Energy
- Data Center Energy
- Computer Energy
- CD Case Production
- CD Production

Research task

In your groups, use the graph to explain how downloading music

a   reduces the carbon footprint of the music industry and

b   makes the music business more efficient.

Record your findings as a presentation or add it to your wiki or website.

Note on the graph *digital = downloading*.

Source: **http://www.treehugger.com/files/2009/10/buying-music-online-can-cut-carbon-emissions-by-80-study-says.php**

Computing technology, the economy and the environment

Using the Internet to help the environment and increase business efficiency

Other ways of using the Internet to help the economy and the environment are telecommuting, teleconferencing, e-commerce, telemedicine and distance learning.

Telecommuting

Many workers have enough bandwidth at home to let them work at home and communicate with their businesses or offices.

Telecommuting reduces greenhouse gases by cutting down the need for travelling to work. Other benefits of using telecommuting for businesses and workers are:

- Reducing travelling costs for employers and workers.
- Increasing efficiency. There is evidence that telecommuters are 40 per cent more productive than their office-based counterparts.
- Making expansion easier: a business can expand without building or renting additional office space or paying for office furniture and equipment.
- Reducing the need for computer equipment. Employees often prefer to use their own computers. This saves the business the cost of buying computer equipment and leads to fewer computers for recycling in the future.

Project 4

Research and report on telecommuting.

Make sure you follow this step-by-step guide:

- Complete a group project planning sheet (see the Appendix on page 144).
- Include a description of telecommuting.
- Produce your report in the form of a slide presentation, a web page or a wiki.
- Include graphics and key points of information.
- Make clear the advantages of using telecommuting for both the environment and the economy.
- Complete individual checklists and questionnaires and a group questionnaire, copies of which you will find in the Appendix.
- Add the following documents to the 'unit2project4' folder in your portfolio: planning sheets, copies of your checklist and questionnaires as well as your presentation or hyperlinks to your wiki or website.

Teleconferencing

Teleconferencing can be used for meetings, interviews and training sessions. It makes businesses and organisations more efficient because it saves on travel time, and on costs such as plane tickets, hotel bills and petrol costs.

Setting up teleconferencing is becoming easier as new technology is developed. Manufacturers are producing Skype-enabled TVs so that you can make video calls and conferences using your HD wide screen TV at home!

This means that if you are working from home you can easily keep in touch with your office as well as your family and friends. An excellent example of computing technology helping the economy and the environment!

Project 5

Research and report on the use of teleconferencing.

Make sure you follow this step-by-step guide:

- Complete a group project planning sheet (see the Appendix on page 144).
- Include a description of teleconferencing.
- Produce your report in the form of a slide presentation, a web page or a wiki.
- Include graphics and key points of information.
- Make clear the advantages of using teleconferencing for both the environment and the economy.
- Complete individual checklists and questionnaires and a group questionnaire, copies of which you will find in the Appendix.
- Add the following documents to the 'unit2project5' folder in your portfolio: planning sheets, copies of your checklist and questionnaires as well as your presentation or hyperlinks to your wiki or website.

Project 6

Research and report on the use of telemedicine in the aftermath of the Haiti earthquake.

Make sure you follow this step-by-step guide:

- Complete a group project planning sheet (see the Appendix on page 144).
- Include a description of telemedicine.
- Produce your report in the form of a slide presentation, a web page or a wiki.
- Include graphics and key points of information.
- Make clear the advantages of using telemedicine.
- Complete individual checklists and questionnaires and a group questionnaire, copies of which you will find in the Appendix.
- Add the following documents to the 'unit2project6' folder in your portfolio: planning sheets, copies of your checklist and questionnaires as well as your presentation or hyperlinks to your wiki or website.

Assessment

Self-assessment

Make sure you have completed all your individual checklists and questionnaires and a group questionnaire for each project. These are available in the Appendix.

Teacher assessment

Your teacher will ask you to place the working files you used to store the information you collected from magazines and the Internet for each project in your portfolio.

If your teacher has access to the dynamic learning materials, you will be asked to complete some online quizzes.

Your teacher will also assess the group's wiki or e-group when you have completed each project as well as how well you have worked as a group.

3

Which security suite?

Why do you need a security suite?

The answer to that question is simple: because there is so much software, known as **malware**, which can damage your computer system or your computer network. There are many different types of malware that can threaten your computer, for example, viruses, worms, trojans, rootkits, scareware, keyloggers, spyware, adware and phishing.

Each of these pose a different type of threat which you should know about.

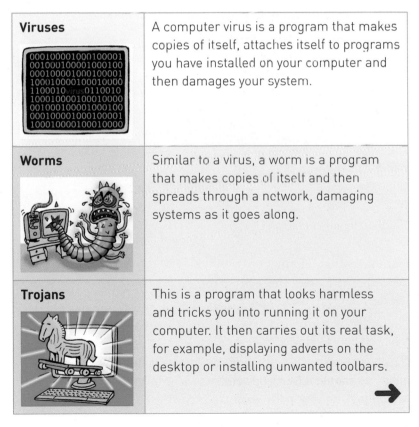

Viruses	A computer virus is a program that makes copies of itself, attaches itself to programs you have installed on your computer and then damages your system.
Worms	Similar to a virus, a worm is a program that makes copies of itself and then spreads through a network, damaging systems as it goes along.
Trojans	This is a program that looks harmless and tricks you into running it on your computer. It then carries out its real task, for example, displaying adverts on the desktop or installing unwanted toolbars. ➡

RAT	A remote access trojan which gives control of your computer to a hacker.
Rootkits	The software that enables a hacker to get control of your computer.
Diallers	A malicious program that takes control of your computer and uses it to dial expensive phone numbers.
Scareware	Scareware is false security software that tries to scare the user into buying it by warning of some threat to the system.
Keylogger	A keylogger is a program designed to track and monitor user keystrokes, often used to steal passwords, credit card numbers, etc.
Spyware	Spyware programs gather information about you from your computer. This can be personal information, or information about which websites you have visited. Some spyware can also change your computer settings.
Adware	Adware displays unwanted adverts on your computer without asking your permission. ➡

Browser exploits	A malicious code that takes advantage of an Internet browser vulnerability to make the browser do something you don't want (freeze, crash, change settings etc.).
Operating system exploits	A malicious code that takes advantage of a weakness in your operating system.
P2P infection	Infected files which come from a file-sharing website.

These next two threats can use keyloggers, trojans, RATs, spyware and even ordinary email to steal your information.

Phishing	Phishing is an attempt to get your personal information such as your bank account details by pretending to be, for example, a charity, or claiming that you have won a cash prize. It's often carried out by email.
Identity theft	When people steal your personal details such as bank account details and pretend to be you, for example, when buying online.

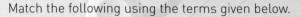
Match the following using the terms given below.

Designed to track and monitor user keystrokes, often used to steal passwords and credit card numbers.	
False security software that tries to frighten the user into buying it.	
A remote access trojan which gives control of your computer to a hacker.	
A program that makes copies of itself and then spreads through a network, damaging systems as it goes along.	
A program that makes copies of itself, attaches itself to programs you have installed on your computer and then damages your system.	
Your system crashes after you have downloaded files from a P2P website.	

Scareware   RAT   P2P infection   keylogger   virus   worm

Progress check!

Name the type of malware at work when:

1 Adverts are constantly appearing on your computer.

2 You install a piece of software because it claims to make your computer work faster, but all sorts of funny things start to happen.

3 Your browser has a design weakness.

4 A business sends you an email stating that you have won £1,000,000. All you have to do is send your bank account details and they will pay it into your account.

5 A piece of software is installed which lets other people control your computer.

Defending against the threats

Security suites

A good security suite will:

- detect and block all of these threats
- have a piece of software called a firewall to stop people and unwanted software from getting into your computer.

Security suites are groups of programs designed to block the threats to your computer. They are divided into two groups: those that are free and those that you have to pay for. The ones that you have to pay for have more features and have more defences built into them.

What is firewall software?

A firewall is a program that has a set of rules that it uses to stop unauthorised access to your computer or network.

Some firewalls are better than others and the websites or magazines you research will let you know if the firewall that is part of a security suite is good enough. For example, companies like Avira and AVG have suite has a free version which offers basic security. The other two versions offer more security which varies according to the price.

Research task

Take a careful look at the features of both the AVG free and payment packages. Visit the website at: **http://free.avg.com/ gb-en/product-comparison**

Now list the features that the free package does not have.

Explain why you would get better protection using one of the paid-for packages.

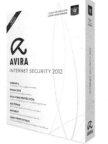

Choosing a security suite

Of course there are lots of security suites out there. A quick search on the Internet will tell you that. The difficulty is in choosing the right suite for your needs.

How do you decide which security suite is best to use?

You need to answer the following questions.

Does the suite protect from every type of threat?

Some suites might not cover every type of threat. The adverts will claim to offer protection, 100 per cent security but it is best to check this out.

How effective is the suite at protecting your computer?

Each security suite claims to protect your computer but does it actually perform as well as it claims? The best way to find out is to look at an online magazine or website that tests the suites and gives them a rating.

How easy is it to use?

Your suite should be easy to download, install, setup and use. If it isn't you might not be able to make full use of it. Security suites are complicated programs but they should be easy for you to use even if you are not an expert!

Does it offer additional support and helpful resources?

Users sometimes need support when they run into a problem. The company that makes the software should give plenty of support, for free! Support can be offered by phone, email, live chatrooms and forums.

How often is it updated?

Security software is only as good as its latest update. New versions of malware are constantly being produced and so, if a security suite is to work properly it needs to be updated each day. If it isn't then it's not going to be of much use!

Research task

Which of these two security suites do you think is the best? You should:

- Read the information in the table below.
- Think about the questions above on pages 45–46.
- Produce a report in which you make your choice, give the reasons for your choice and explain why you rejected the other one.

Panther security 1.8	Defender 8.4
Panther gives protection from viruses, worms, trojans and spyware.	Defender protects from viruses, worms, trojans and spyware, keyloggers, phishing scams, email-borne threats and rootkits.
Once installed, it runs by itself.	User has to change settings using the menus supplied.
Updates automatically every day.	Updates when the user requests it.
Stopped 80 per cent of malware when tested.	Stopped 95 per cent of malware when tested.

Research task

Which of these three security suites do you think is the best?

Read the information in the table below, think about the questions above on pages 45–46, make your choice, then produce a report in which you give the reasons for your choice and explain why you rejected the other two.

Walls security 3	Alert 2.1	Police 9.11
Protects from viruses, worms, trojans and spyware, keyloggers, phishing scams, email-borne threats and rootkits.	Gives protection from viruses, worms, trojans, RATs, adware and spyware.	Protects from viruses, worms, trojans and spyware, keyloggers, phishing scams, RATs, email-borne threats and rootkits.
A complex program which installs and runs automatically.	Installs and runs automatically.	To install this suite the user has to change settings using the menus supplied.
Updates automatically once every day.	Updates as soon as a new threat is discovered.	Updates on request.
Stopped 80 per cent of malware when tested.	Stopped 65 per cent of malware when tested	Stopped 90 per cent of malware when tested.
Has free support and help using email.	Has free support and help using email and chat rooms.	Has support and help using phone lines charged at 50p per minute.
Costs £42 per year.	Free.	£30 per year.

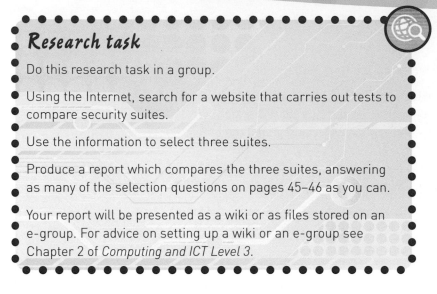

Research task

Do this research task in a group.

Using the Internet, search for a website that carries out tests to compare security suites.

Use the information to select three suites.

Produce a report which compares the three suites, answering as many of the selection questions on pages 45–46 as you can.

Your report will be presented as a wiki or as files stored on an e-group. For advice on setting up a wiki or an e-group see Chapter 2 of *Computing and ICT Level 3*.

Remember to follow the steps on pages 23–25 when tackling the group project. Here are some examples to help you with steps 1, 3 and 4 of your project.

Step 1: Group project planning sheet

Here is an example of a group project planning sheet which has been completed to guide you.

Task of each person in the group	Jean will use the search engine to find information on one security suite and choose useful information. Alex will search for a website that compares security suites and send its address to each member of the group. He will then collect all the information files from the group. Gregor will use a search engine to find useful information on one security suite. Margaret will check out the school's PC magazine articles for useful information.
Sources of information	Websites and PC magazine articles.
Recording information	All useful information will be stored in note form in word processing files. Each person in the group will send their completed files to Alex.
Group communication	We will use meetings in class, email and our wiki which will have a to-do page. ➡

How our information will be presented	We will use a wiki. Alex will set up the home page with links to pages for each member of the group.
	Each person in the group will then add their information to their pages, with Alex's help.
	We will then have a meeting to decide on what to put in the comparison section of the report.
Time plan with target deadlines	Lesson 1: complete the group project planning sheet.
	Lessons 2, 3, & 4: do the research, select the key information and record it in a word processing file and send it to Alex.
	Lessons 5 & 6: set up the wiki.
	Lesson 7: discuss what to put in the comparison section and complete the wiki.
	Lesson 8: fill in the assessment sheets.
	Lesson 9: present the wiki to the class and our teacher.

A blank copy of this group project planning sheet is in the Appendix on page 144 and is available as part of the Dynamic Learning resource package (see **www.dynamic-learning.co.uk**).

Step 3: Start the research

Once you have completed your group project planning sheet it is time to begin the research. This website should help you:
http://Internet-security-suite-review.toptenreviews.com/

Step 4: Produce the report

Here is a sample report to guide you.

Research task sample report

Norton	Bullguard	G Data
Has all the software needed to block threats from, e.g. adware, spyware, trojans, viruses etc. This protection software has a top rating when tested.	Has all the software needed to block threats from, e.g. adware, spyware, trojans, viruses etc. But its software does not have a top rating when tested.	Has anti-spyware and anti-virus protection but it is not completely effective. It doesn't detect adware, keyloggers or browser exploits. It doesn't have identity protection or P2P protection.
Has a very good firewall with a top rating.	Its firewall is not given a top rating.	Its firewall is not given a top rating.
Has lots of support from email, phone, chatroom, manuals and FAQs.	Has lots of support from email, chatroom, manuals and FAQs but no phone-based support.	The only support it has is by using email and an FAQ web page.
It is very easy to use.	It is not that easy to use.	It is not that easy to use.
It has automatic updates.	It has automatic updates.	It doesn't have automatic updates.
Cost = £49	Cost = £40	Cost = £22

Comparison

Protecting from threats

The best of these three security suites is the Norton because it has all the software needed to stop the threats to my computer and this software is given a top rating which means it worked very well when it was tested.

The Bullguard software does not have a top rating and the G Data has lots of protection missing.

Firewall

The Norton is the only one with a top-rated firewall. This means that the other two would not be able to stop all unwanted access to my computer.

Support

Norton has every type of support and the Bullguard has no phone support. G Data only has email support.

Ease of use

Norton is the easiest suite to use and has automatic updates which G Data does not.

Cost

Norton costs the most at £49.

Recommendation

Norton costs the most at £49 but I would still recommend it because it gives the best protection and support.

Assessment

Self-assessment

Make sure you have completed all your individual checklists and questionnaires and a group questionnaire for each project. These are available in the Appendix at the back of the book.

Teacher assessment

Your teacher will ask you to place the working files you used to store the information you collected from magazines and the Internet for each project in your portfolio.

If your teacher has access to the Dynamic Learning materials, you will be asked to complete some online quizzes.

Your teacher will also assess the group's wiki or e-group when you have completed each project as well as how well you have worked as a group.

4

An introduction to programming using Scratch

Creativity lies at the heart of the success of the human race. It is our ability to create that has allowed us to develop civilisations and to share the wealth of human experience across the ages.

Creativity takes many forms. Musicians create tunes and lyrics that provide a soundtrack to our lives. Artists capture or make images in many forms to enrich, delight, challenge and amuse.

One area of creativity in our modern world is in the creation of computer games. The talents of many people go into creating a successful game. The backgrounds and characters need to be detailed, distinctive and eye-catching. The music has to be exciting and match the mood of the game. However it is the **programmer** that lies at the heart of every game!

We are going to look at programming in this chapter. For this we are going to use a freeware[1] programming language called **Scratch**. The language was developed at the Massachusetts Institute of Technology (MIT) in the United States to teach programming skills to young people in a very visual way. You can download your own copy of Scratch from their website; just go to your favourite search engine and type 'Scratch MIT'.

Projects, sprites, costumes and scripts

Programs in Scratch are called **projects**. A project can have one or more characters in it and these are called **sprites**. You can make a sprite look like anything you want. It can be a cartoon icon, a photo, clip art or anything else. Once you are used to Scratch, try creating your own sprites in a drawing package.

---

[1] Freeware means that you can download and use the software for free for as long as you like. You can give the program to anyone else, but you **cannot** sell it and you must not change it or pretend you created it.

A sprite can look different in different parts of the program, depending on what is happening. Think about the characters in games on handheld consoles like the Nintendo DS™ or Wii™. Each version of a sprite is called a **costume**. Flicking between costumes can make a sprite look like it is running, swimming, flying or jumping.

You tell each sprite what to do – to move around the screen or react to other sprites. The instructions look like little building blocks and are grouped together in the panel on the left of the window.

Each set of instructions for a sprite is called a **script** in Scratch. Scripts are created by clicking these instruction blocks together. Scripts are run from top to bottom. To run a script just click on it or click the green flag at the top of the screen.

The script below is a short quiz. Read it carefully and see if you can figure out what each part does. Don't worry if you can't get it all, we will be showing you how to create this quiz later.

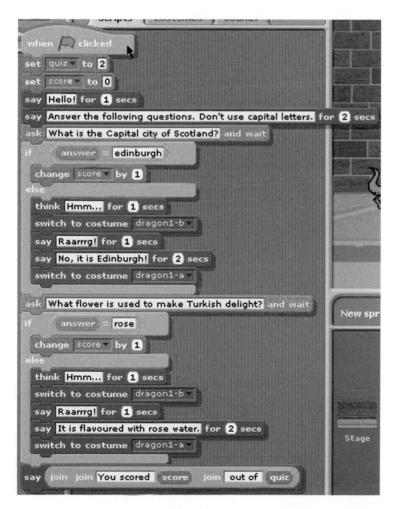

Below is a screenshot of the main Scratch window you will see when you launch the program.

The screen is split up into a number of **panels**.

The top right panel is the **stage**. This is where all the action takes place. Here sprites appear, move and interact with each other. You can give it any background picture you like. Clicking the green flag at the top right of this panel will run the project. Click the red octagon to stop the script.

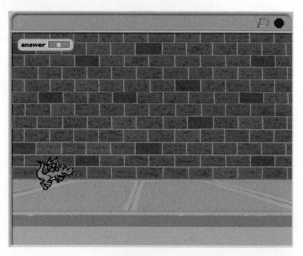

The panel on the bottom right shows **all** the sprites in the project, we are using a dragon in this one. Clicking on one of the three 'new sprite' buttons will allow you to create a new sprite, choose a sprite from the extensive sprite collection or get Scratch to surprise you with one it chooses!

Clicking on the **Stage** icon lets you create or import a new background for the action to happen in front of. We have chosen the brick wall from the large list of backgrounds within Scratch. If you don't like what is on offer you can edit a background or even use a digital photograph.

The **scripts** area is where you will tell each sprite what to do by dragging instructions across from the left and clicking them together.

The current sprite is shown at the top, a dragon here. This is the character that will carry out the instructions shown in the panel.

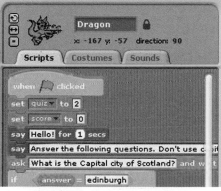

By clicking on the costumes tab in the script area you can choose, create or edit **costumes** for your sprite. Costumes make sprites look more interactive.

The **blocks palette** is where the instructions, or blocks, are listed.
There are eight types of block, for doing different kinds of things.
They are colour coded to make life easier! Below are all the blocks
that you can use to program your sprites. We will only use **some** of
them in this book.

Motion   Control
Looks   Sensing
Sound   Operators
Pen   Variables

move 10 steps
turn 15 degrees
turn 15 degrees

point in direction 90
point towards

go to x: 0 y: 0
go to
glide 1 secs to x: 0 y: 0

change x by 10
set x to 0
change y by 10
set y to 0

if on edge, bounce

x position
y position
direction

clear

pen down
pen up

set pen color to
change pen color by 10
set pen color to 0

change pen shade by 10
set pen shade to 50

change pen size by 1
set pen size to 1

stamp

play sound meow
play sound meow until done
stop all sounds

play drum 48 for 0.2 beats
rest for 0.2 beats

play note 60 for 0.5 beats
set instrument to 1

change volume by -10
set volume to 100 %
volume

change tempo by 20
set tempo to 60 bpm
tempo

switch to costume costume2
next costume
costume #

say Hello! for 2 secs
say Hello!
think Hmm... for 2 secs
think Hmm...

change color effect by 25
set color effect to 0
clear graphic effects

change size by 10
set size to 100 %
size

show
hide

go to front
go back 1 layers

when clicked

when space key pressed

when Sprite1 clicked

wait 1 secs

forever

repeat 10

broadcast
broadcast and wait

when I receive

forever if

if

if
else

wait until

repeat until

stop script
stop all

+
-
*
/

pick random 1 to 10

<
=
>

and
or
not

join hello world
letter 1 of world
length of world

mod
round

sqrt of 10

touching ?
touching color ?
color is touching ?

ask What's your name? and wait
answer

mouse x
mouse y
mouse down?

key space pressed?

distance to

reset timer
timer

x position of Sprite1

loudness
loud?

slider sensor value
sensor button pressed ?

Making the crab talk

The first thing we need to do is to open a new project in Scratch. We are going to need a fishy background, which we get by clicking on the stage icon and importing a background. Here we will use the 'underwater' background from the 'nature' collection. Next we need to import a suitable sprite. The red crab (crab1-b) from the 'Animals' collection seems ideal.

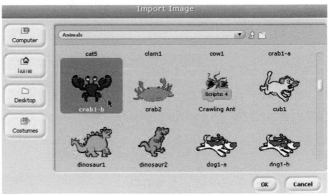

You should delete the cat sprite by right-clicking and choosing delete.

The project should now look like this:

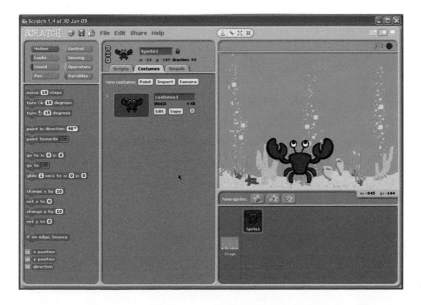

Now we have to write a couple of scripts to make the sprite do something interesting.

We want the crab to:

- say hello
- crawl to the other side of the stage
- ask your name
- say goodbye to you.

For this we will use the blocks on the right.

The order that the blocks go in is very important. This is the order that Scratch will carry out the instructions. Below is the final script, with a description of what each block does.

Start the script when the green flag is clicked.

- Make the sprite say 'Hello!'
- Get the crab to ask your name. A box appears for the reply, which is stored in 'answer'.
- Slide the crab across the bottom of the screen.
- Add 'hello' and the answer together and say it.

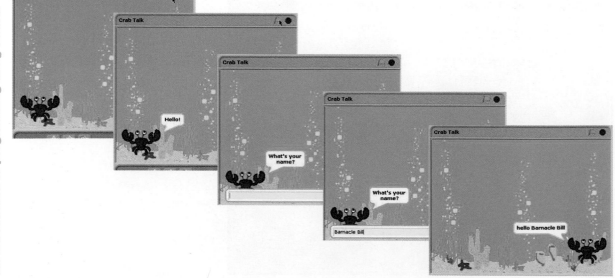

Dancing crustaceans!

To experiment with some of the other motion blocks and a repeat, look at this set of blocks for our crabby friend. We have set the start point for the crab and given it a simple dance move!

What do you think will happen when we run the script?

Project tasks

Try creating the crab project above, entering each of the crab scripts and running them to see what they do.

Edit the script by changing the values in the white boxes. Notice how the new values change what happens when the script is run.

Try editing the project to change the sprite and the background. Make it say or ask other things. Make sure that you keep track of the order of blocks.

Wizard with tables!

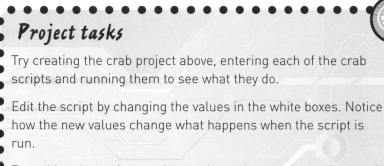

Here is a project that does multiplication tables.

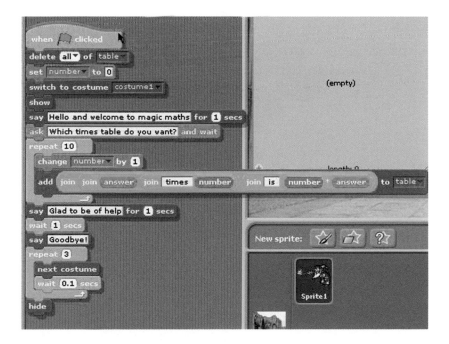

It uses a **table** to gather the results together and show them.

It also uses multiple costumes and **show/hide** to give the illusion that the wizard disappears at the end of the script!

Project tasks

Try creating the above project. Discuss what the first couple of lines in the script are for with your teacher/group.

Edit the project to turn it into a currency calculator.

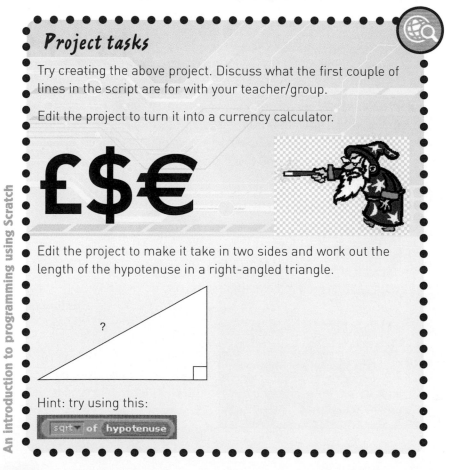

Edit the project to make it take in two sides and work out the length of the hypotenuse in a right-angled triangle.

Hint: try using this:

`sqrt ▾ of hypotenuse`

Looping the loops

If you look at the **control** block used inside the crab and wizard projects, you will see that a **fixed loop** has been used to make the script repeat a series of actions.

The other type of loop that can be used is the **conditional loop**. Here the blocks in the loop are repeated a number of times. The loop only stops when a condition is met. You use a **conditional loop** when you do not know how often you want to repeat a series of actions. The **conditions** can be found in the **operators** section.

There are several different types of condition block.

You can combine conditions so that the loop repeats until:

(condition A) **AND** (condition B) are both **true**

(condition X) is **NOT true**

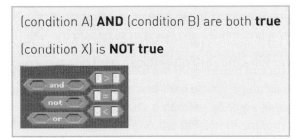

Setting limits with input validation

You can use conditions to protect your scripts from the user entering wrong data.

The script on the right can be used in a project to make sure that the variable called **number** ends up with a **positive** value.

This is called **input validation**.

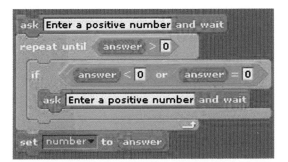

Sliding to the edge

Another way to protect your scripts from the user entering the wrong data is to use a **slider**. This technique means that the user can only enter numbers in a given range, as set by the programmer when he or she creates the slider.

Here is how to create a slider for a variable in a script:

Create your variable (we have gone for Computing Grade).

Computing Grade 0

Make it visible on the stage.

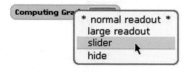

Right-click and choose 'slider'.

Right-click again and set the 'min and max'.

Slider range:

Min: 1   Max: 9

OK   Cancel

You now have a slider with whole numbers in the given range!

Computing Grade 3

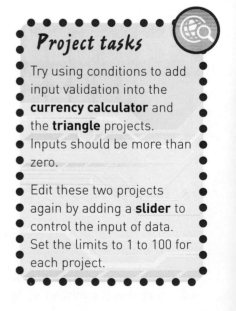

Project tasks

Try using conditions to add input validation into the **currency calculator** and the **triangle** projects. Inputs should be more than zero.

Edit these two projects again by adding a **slider** to control the input of data. Set the limits to 1 to 100 for each project.

Quizzing the dragon

Now we are going to have a go at creating the dragon quiz from the start of the chapter.

First we need a new **project**. Delete the cat sprite and choose the dragon as your **sprite**.

There will be two **costumes** ('dragon1-a' and 'dragon1-b' from the sprite bank).

The **stage** will be the brick wall.

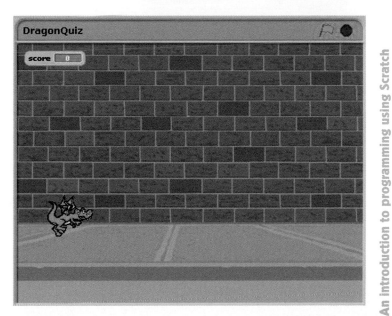

Next we have to think about **how** we are going to write the **script** for the quiz. There are a few steps to carry out to solve the problem. Here is a basic plan (or algorithm):

- Start the script.
- Set the score variable to zero.
- Set the total number of questions.
- Give some instructions.
- Ask a question.
- If the answer typed is correct:
    Add one to the score.
- Otherwise:
    Change to the angry dragon costume.
    Say 'Roar' and the correct answer.
    Change to starting dragon costume.
- End the 'if' block.
- Duplicate steps 5 to 12 for each question.
- Say how many scored correct out of the total.

Step 1: Use the 'green flag' block to start the script.

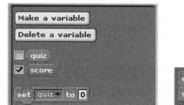

Steps 2 and 3: Set up two variables (ours are 'quiz' and 'score', as that made sense to us). You need to have score visible (click the box). Set score to 0 and quiz to the total number of questions (we made it 2).

Step 4: Give the user some instructions. Use the 'say' block to say 'Hello' and ask the user not to use capitals. *We* know that 'Edinburgh' means the same thing as 'edinburgh', but it just confuses things for the computer!

Step 5: Use the 'ask' block to ask a question.

The user will type their answer into the box on the screen and it will be stored in the 'answer' variable.

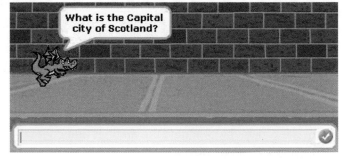

Step 6: To make a **decision** in a script, you need to use a control block. We need the 'if...else...' block.

We also need to compare two things using the equals operator.

Step 7: If the user gives the correct answer, we need to do the first set of instructions in the 'if' block (the first branch) and add one to the score.

Step 8 to 12: Otherwise, if the user is wrong, we need to do the second branch of the 'if' block and get the angry dragon to tell them the correct answer.

Step 13: To say the answer we used the 'say' block, *three* copies of the 'join' operator and our two variables.

This looks quite complicated, as we wanted to build a proper sentence. You could just as easily have said something like 'Hey, the number of correct answers was x'. Then you would only have needed one 'join'.

Steps 5 to 12 have to be copied for *each* of the questions in the quiz. You just need to edit the parts with the question and answers. You can have as many questions as you like.

Try creating the previous project for yourself. Enter the two questions in the script and run the project. Discuss it with your teacher/group. Does it do what it is meant to? Is there a better way of solving the problem?

Edit the project by changing the number and content of the questions. Change the background, sprite and costumes.

Try working in groups to create a themed quiz. Perhaps a plant could ask 10 revision questions about biology or a robot could test your ICT knowledge. Get creative!

If you are working in larger groups, test out each other's quizzes. Discuss what is good about each quiz. Find one thing to improve in your quiz and change it.

Try putting the whole quiz inside a conditional loop. At the end of the questions, tell the user the score and ask if they want to play again (Y/N). Only let the quiz finish if they reply 'N', otherwise loop back to the start and reset the score.

Ghosthunter – a simple game

The next project we will look at is a simple game that will use motion and mouse control.

The game will involve you, as a knight, chasing a ghost around the screen until you have caught the ghost 20 times. You will need to choose a suitable background picture; we have gone for a school corridor.

Next you need the sprites. Sprite one will be the ghost. It will have two costumes that it will swap between.

Sprite two is our valiant knight!

All three are to be found in the sprite library.

You should end up with a screen much like the one on the right.

Next you will need to write the scripts to control each sprite.

The knight will follow the following steps:

- Start the script.
- Set the score variable to zero.
- Loop while score < 20:
    Glide to where the mouse is pointing.
    If it is touching the ghost:
        add 1 to the score.
        move away.
- If the score = 20:
    Say 'Victory!'
    Stop all scripts.

You can see the finished script on the right.

The ghost is slightly more complicated as it has to run around avoiding the knight.

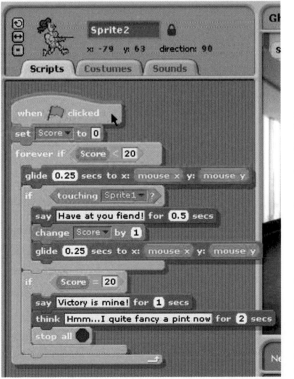

It will follow the following steps:

- Start the script.
- Make the sprite appear.
- Loop forever:
    Glide to a random point.
    Switch costume.
    'Moan' at the knight.
    Glide to a random point.
    Switch costume.
    'Boo' at the knight.
    If score = 20 hide the sprite.
- End loop.

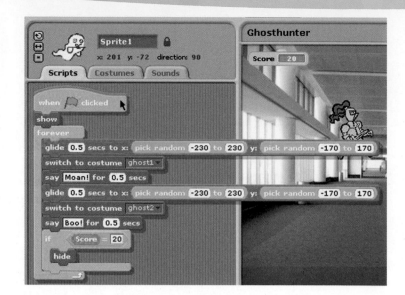

You can see the plan of the script on the left above and the finished script on the right. The script will only stop running when stopped in the knight's script, that is, when the score is 20. Most of the blocks are familiar to you by now, the only part that might need some explanation is the 'pick random' instruction in the glide block. This will choose a random number in a given range.

This point is a set of randomly generated co-ordinates.

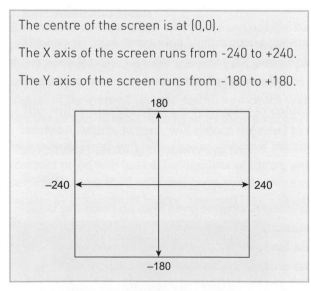

The centre of the screen is at (0,0).

The X axis of the screen runs from -240 to +240.

The Y axis of the screen runs from -180 to +180.

The script will use 'pick random' to choose an X co-ordinate between -230 and +230 and a Y co-ordinate between -170 and +170.

We then get the ghost to slide/glide along to the chosen point on the screen in half a second. Now the chase is on!

Create the above project and run it. Change some of the parameters in the scripts and run it again. Discuss the effect of the changes with your teacher/group. Adapt the game to suit yourself. Try using a sprite hand to swat flies – anything you like!

Music maestro please

Here is a script that plays some music when the flag is clicked.

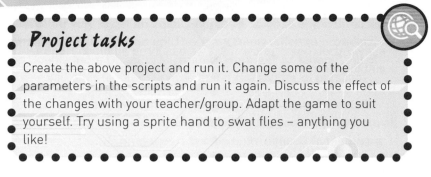

The blocks used set the instrument (here it is instrument 13, a mighty marimba!), the tempo (the speed the music is played at, here 55 beats per minute) and the note played (the first note is 53, an F) and how many beats it plays for.

```
(1) Acoustic Grand
(2) Bright Acoustic
(3) Electric Grand
(4) Honky-Tonk
(5) Electric Piano 1
(6) Electric Piano 2
(7) Harpsichord
(8) Clavinet
(9) Celesta
(10) Glockenspiel
(11) Music Box
(12) Vibraphone
(13) Marimba
(14) Xylophone
(15) Tubular Bells
(16) Dulcimer
(17) Drawbar Organ
(18) Percussive Organ
(19) Rock Organ
```

If you can read music, or get someone to write the notes down for you, you can get really creative!

Project tasks

Try creating the script above and playing the music.

Change the instrument and the tempo in the script and run it again. Discuss the effect of the changes with your teacher/group.

Work in groups to create a couple of tunes in each group. Try out other tunes in the class. Choose a background and put a few sprites on it. Attach a tune to each sprite. Remember to use the 'when sprite clicked' block to activate it. Now you have a music game. Just click on any sprite to play its music.

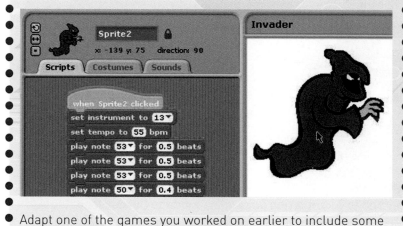

Adapt one of the games you worked on earlier to include some music. In your groups, discuss whether you think that adding music to the game makes it better.

Dragon maths – adding value to sums

Now we are going to create a simple game to help teach basic addition to younger gamers.

We are going to use the bricks background again and a dragon sprite to ask the questions.

First we have to think carefully about how we are going to write the script for the dragon.

Here is a basic algorithm (or plan):

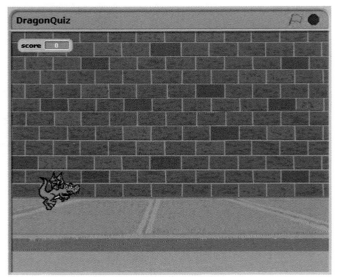

- Start the script.
- Set the score variable to zero.
- Set the total number of questions.
- Give some instructions.
- Ask a question (What is X plus Y?).
- If the answer typed is correct:
    Add one to the score.
- Otherwise:
    Change to angry dragon costume.
    Say 'Roar' and the correct answer.
    Change to starting dragon costume.
- Duplicate steps 5 to 7 for each question.
- Say how many scored correct out of the total.

It looks simple, but there are a lot of steps.

First we have to create a number of variables, one for each of the two numbers to be added, one for the result, one for the number of questions and one for the score! We have chosen to show the two numbers and the score on the stage – you might just want to see the score.

We will set the quiz to 10, because we want to ask 10 questions. We will set the initial values of first, second and score to zero. We will also get the dragon to say 'Hello!', because that's the polite thing to do!

We want first and second to be a random number between 1 and 10. The result is these two added together.

```
set first to pick random 1 to 10
set second to pick random 1 to 10
set result to first + second
```

The next step is to ask the question.

```
ask join join What is first join plus second and wait
```

When the user types the answer we make the script compare this to the calculated result and change the score by 1 or get the dragon to breathe fire.

```
if answer = result
    change score by 1
else
    think Hmm... for 1 secs
    switch to costume dragon1-b
    say Raarrrg! for 2 secs
    switch to costume dragon1-a
```

Dragon
x: -167 y: -57 direction: 90

Scripts | Costumes | Sounds

New costume: Paint | Import | Camera

1   dragon1-a
    64x58   3 KB
    Edit Copy ⊗

2   dragon1-b
    103x66   3 KB
    Edit Copy ⊗

After the loop in the script has been repeated 10 times (value of the quiz), we will get the dragon to say the score.

```
repeat quiz
```

```
say join join You scored score join out of quiz
```

The complete screen is shown here.

Assessment

Self-assessment

Make sure you have completed all your individual checklists and questionnaires and a group questionnaire for each project. These are available in the Appendix at the back of the book.

Teacher assessment

Your teacher will ask you to place the working files you used to store the information you collected from magazines and the Internet for each project in your portfolio.

If your teacher has access to the dynamic learning materials, you will be asked to complete some online quizzes.

Your teacher will also assess the group's wiki or e-group when you have completed each project as well as how well you have worked as a group.

Project tasks

Create the above project and run it. Change the parameters, like the number of questions in the quiz or the range of the random number and run it again. Discuss the effect of the changes with your teacher/group.

Adapt the maths game by making a multiplication quiz. You could combine it with the earlier quiz program to ask more difficult maths questions!

5

Graphics and animations

In this chapter we will look at graphics and animations. There is a huge range of software out there to do this kind of thing, ranging from freeware to some very expensive professional applications. A couple of examples of freeware that can do a similar range of tasks are OpenOffice.org™ Draw and GIMP – just shop around for one that suits you. You don't have to spend a fortune – but you could if you really wanted to!

Graphics

For graphics we will be using a version of Serif DrawPlus™. This graphics package is part of a very powerful, and popular, suite of applications from Serif. This software is not free, but carries quite a lot of powerful features for the price. (There is a freeware version but many of the screens will look different to those mentioned here.)

Getting started with Serif DrawPlus™

Open up the package at first and you will see the start-up screen, shown on the right.

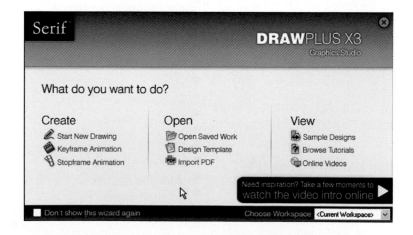

It gives you a number of choices, including animation, which we will get to later.

Choose 'Start new drawing' and you will get the screen below.

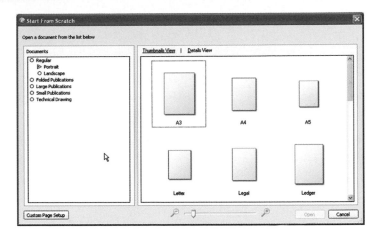

This lets you select the paper size that you will be working in.

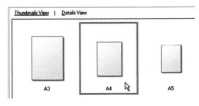

We want regular A4, the usual size of a sheet of paper in the UK. We also want the page to be longer vertically, called portrait, rather than on its side, called landscape.

Now we are ready to do some actual drawing. Let's play around with the basic features of the package before getting to the more powerful tools. The basic screen looks like this.

You can see the main page, often called the 'drawing canvas'. There is a tool bar down the left side. In Serif DrawPlus™, the main tools are as below, but you get similar things in other packages.

Pointer tool		Used for selecting and manipulating objects.
Node tool		Used for distorting shapes by dragging nodes around.
Pencil		Used for drawing thinner freehand lines.
Paintbrush		Used for wider freehand lines and effects.
Pen		Used for drawing curved lines.
Straight line		Used for drawing straight lines.
Freeform paint tool		Used for producing other brush effects, like eraser and knife.
Quick shapes		Used for adding in a variety of standard shapes.
Artistic text		Used for adding text or text art.
Insert picture		Used for inserting pictures.

We will look at some of these tools in detail during the chapter, but the best way to learn any package is often to jump straight in and play around a bit!

Drawing simple graphics using Quick shapes

The Quick shapes palette allows us quickly to produce a wide variety of standard shapes.

We are going to use this tool to draw a heart. Select the heart shape from the palette and click on the drawing canvas, dragging across it to draw the heart. As you drag the pointer across the canvas, you will see the dimensions of the shape displayed along its edges.

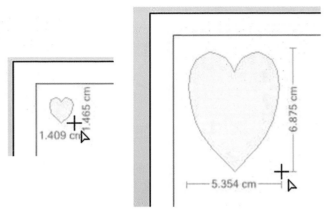

When you let go of the mouse button, boxes will appear around the shape. These 'handles' allow you to resize the shape.

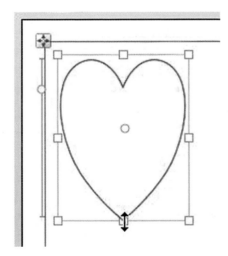

If you use the pointer tool to 'grab' a handle at the top, bottom or one of the sides and drag it around, you can stretch and distort the shape.

If you grab the handles at the corners you can make the shape bigger without distorting it. To move the shape around the canvas, just grab the middle of the shape and drag it to where you want it to be.

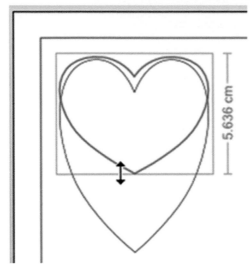

Now it is time to have a go.

Open up Serif DrawPlus™, or whatever you are using, and start with a blank A4 canvas in portrait.

Project tasks

Draw a few basic shapes using the Quick shapes tool. Swap to the pointer tool and move them around. Grab the handles and stretch each of them, making them tall and thin or short and wide.

Use a few basic shapes to create a design for a dinner plate. Here's an example.

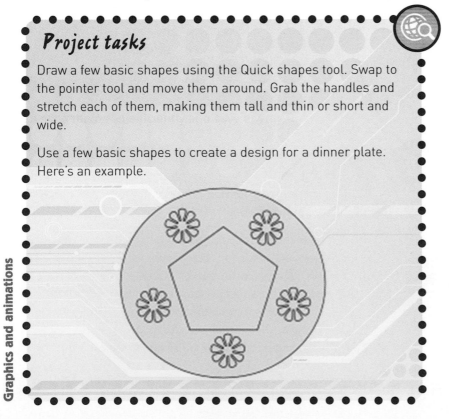

Copying or duplicating shapes

The example in the dinner plate task used duplicate flower shapes in the design. You can get this effect quickly if you draw one shape and use copy and paste, usually found in the edit menu of a draw package or in the tool bar.

Just click on the shape you want to duplicate and choose copy; this will put a copy on the clipboard. Then click on paste and drag the copy to where you want it.

Rotating shapes

Another use for the handles is to turn, or rotate, the shapes. Just move the pointer tool near the corner handle and you will see a little double-headed arrow appear. Now just click and drag to spin the shape.

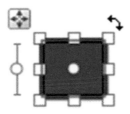

Getting out of the black!

Now it is time to start choosing colours for shapes. You will see the colour wheel on the right of the drawing canvas. Click on a shape and drag the coloured corner round to point at the colour you want. The tiny circle in the triangle shows the colour you have chosen. The nearer this is to the black corner, the darker the colour and the nearer this is to the white corner, the lighter it is.

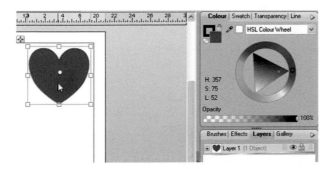

If we have another look at the plate design, we can add some colours to it.

Project tasks

Use the Quick shapes tool to draw a simple house. You should have a door, four windows and a roof. Use some colours in your design.

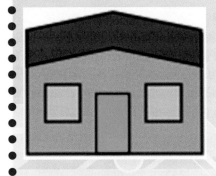

Use the shield shape to design and create a coat of arms. Try a couple of simple designs first. If you have a school badge, you might like to try to copy that!

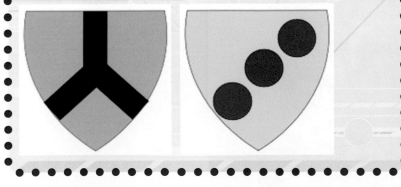

Distorting shapes by using sliders

As we have already seen, when you create a shape there are handles around it that you can use to resize it. There are also sliders on each shape that let you affect how it looks.

If we draw a heart, there is a slider on the left side. This controls just how deep the 'notch' at the tip of the heart is.

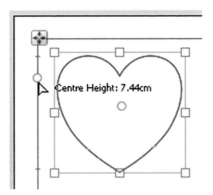

If you drag the slider down the heart will distort, eventually looking like a pair of insect wings!

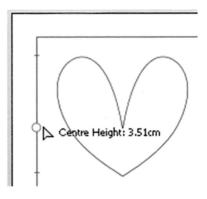

The slider on a rectangle affects how rounded the corners are. Dragging it up gives you a rounded rectangle; the corners eventually get so rounded that the square is actually a circle! Dragging the slider down rounds the corners the other way, giving you a sort of cross shape.

There are two sliders on a circle.

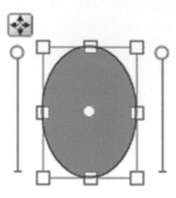

The one on the left controls how big a slice you cut out of it and the one on the right controls where that slice starts.

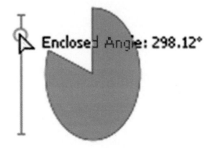

Enclosed Angle: 298.12°

By moving both sliders we can create a smiling Martian head!

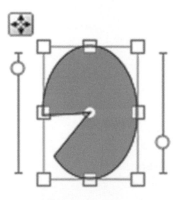

Project tasks

Use the Quick petal tool and the sliders to create this circular saw blade.

Use the Quick face tool and the slider to create this miserable chap.

Use the Quick spiral tool and the sliders to create this piece of jewellery.

Use the Quick clock tool and the sliders to show that it is time to go home!

Use the Quick star tool and the sliders to create this company logo.

Use the Quick web tool and the sliders to create this logo of a web.

Drawing lines

Serif DrawPlus™ can help you create almost any kind of line you can imagine and probably a few that you didn't!

The Line tool is on the tool bar on the left-hand side of the screen, but the bit of the software that makes lines really interesting is the Line tab. You will see it over on the right of the drawing canvas beside the Transparency tab.

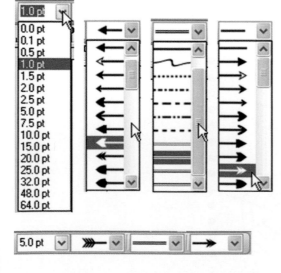

Here you can control three things:

- the line thickness, measured in points
- the shape of each of the two ends
- the shape of the middle of the line.

Project tasks

Use the Line tool and the Line tab to create this arrow.

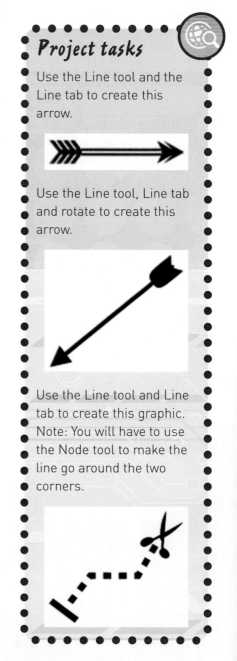

Use the Line tool, Line tab and rotate to create this arrow.

Use the Line tool and Line tab to create this graphic. Note: You will have to use the Node tool to make the line go around the two corners.

Things may appear larger

Once your graphics get more complicated, you may want to work on finer detail. The Navigator panel is on the bottom right of the screen.

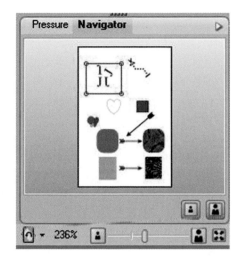

The 'Fit page' button zooms the whole page to make it fit exactly on one screen.

The slider allows you to zoom in or out.

You can drag the red box around the navigator to show different parts of the page on the drawing canvas. Below is an example of how to zoom in on the detail of a page.

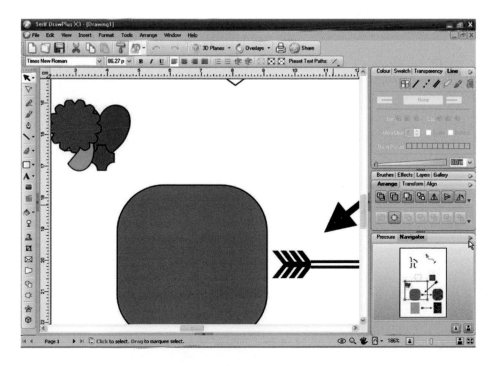

Objects and layers

Each shape, or object, that you draw is placed on a different layer. The first object drawn is on the bottom layer. The next object sits on top of that. As the objects build up, they overlap.

The Arrange toolbar allows you to change the order of the objects. It also allows you to flip or rotate the objects.

Move to front

Forward one

Back one

Move to back

Flip horizontal

Flip vertical

Rotate 30°

To change the order of objects, simply click on the object you want to shift up or down and click the button. The best way of seeing how this works is to draw a few objects and swap them around.

Project tasks

Draw four shapes like those on the right.

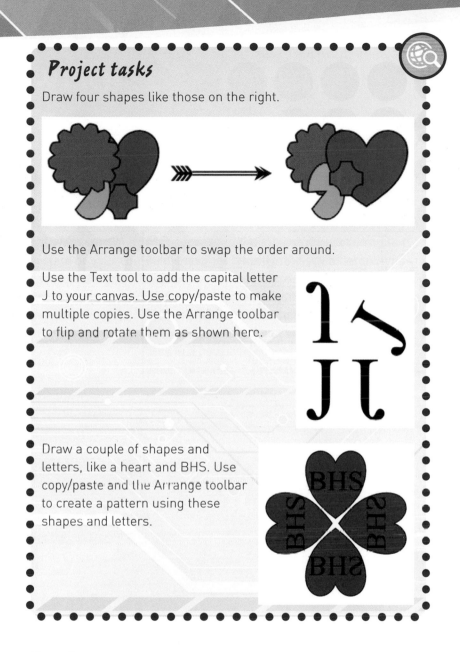

Use the Arrange toolbar to swap the order around.

Use the Text tool to add the capital letter J to your canvas. Use copy/paste to make multiple copies. Use the Arrange toolbar to flip and rotate them as shown here.

Draw a couple of shapes and letters, like a heart and BHS. Use copy/paste and the Arrange toolbar to create a pattern using these shapes and letters.

More about text

We sneaked some text into the exercises above; now let's look at text properly. The Text tool works as you would expect. Click on the Artistic text button on the button bar.

A ▾ | A | Artistic Text
    | | Frame Text

This will help you add in a section of what Serif DrawPlus™ calls Artistic text.

Just drag the cursor to the size you want and type in the text you want.

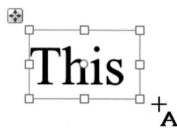

The Text menu bar shows the font, the size and some of the usual style and alignment options.

It also gives you the option of changing the text path. The normal text path is straight across, but there are several pre-set text paths to choose from – with some very interesting results!

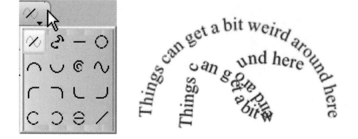

If you create text you can use the colour wheel and line thickness to create some interesting effects.

Red and Blue

Project tasks

Create the 'red and blue' logo on page 88. You can use your own font, size and colours if you like.

Create this logo using copy and paste. You can use your own font if you like.

A quick way to edit the text is to right click on the text and then choose 'Text' and 'Edit text'.

Use the pre-set text paths to create this logo for a well-known team of textbook writers!

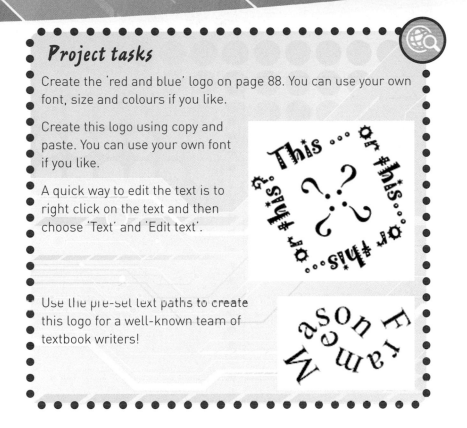

The other type of text tool is Frame text. This is used for larger blocks of text as described below.

You might have a lot of text to include in your document, such as instructions on a help sheet or the steps in a recipe. For this you should choose Frame text. This creates a text box that you can type, or just paste, a block of text into. If there is too much text for the box, an 'overflow' tag is shown. Click on this to shrink the text to fit perfectly inside the box.

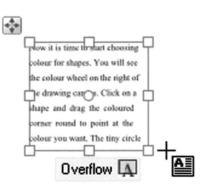

The text box can be rotated by hovering at the corner of the text box until the rotate tag appears. You can then drag it round to the angle that you want.

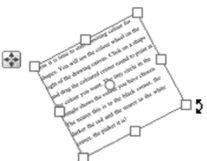

Project tasks

Use blocks of Frame text to make up a help sheet on one of the previous lessons. Your sheet should include step-by-step instructions and diagrams.

If you are working in a larger class, try working in pairs on different help sheets. This will give the class a great learning resource as well!

Choose a poem, or very short story, and use the text tools to make it 'flow' down the page.

Create and add some relevant drawings as illustrations to improve the look of the page.

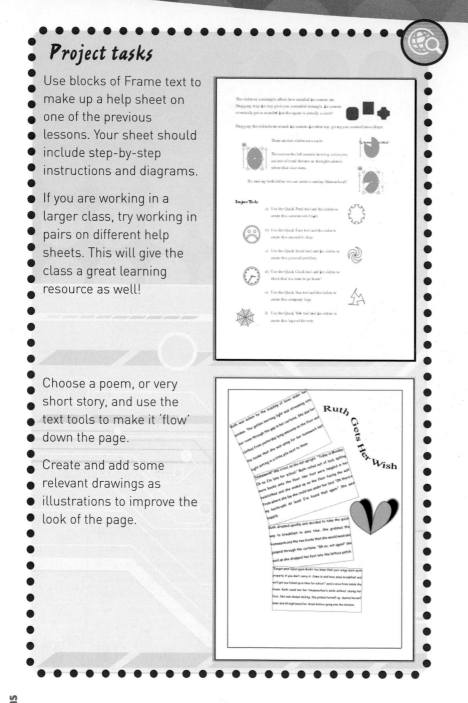

Opacity/transparency

Another way to manipulate objects is to change their opacity, or transparency. This means that you are able to see one object through another one on top of it.

Take the four objects on the right.

First we click on the top shape, here it is the flower shape.

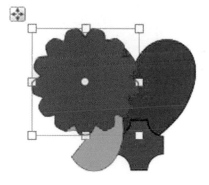

Then we drag the opacity slider, below the colour wheel, along to around 35%.

Opacity	
▓▓▓▓▓▓▓▓	61%

We repeat this with another shape on the top.

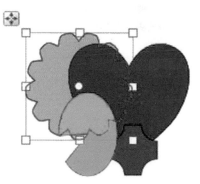

Try this yourself to see how it works.

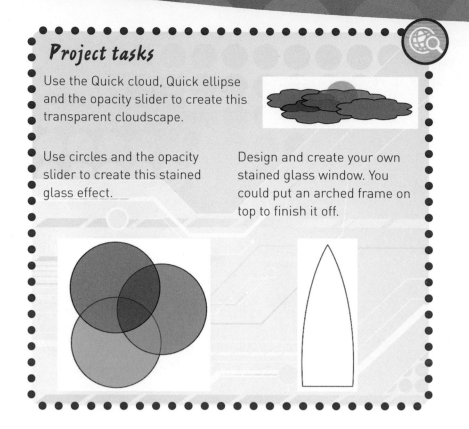

Project tasks

Use the Quick cloud, Quick ellipse and the opacity slider to create this transparent cloudscape.

Use circles and the opacity slider to create this stained glass effect.

Design and create your own stained glass window. You could put an arched frame on top to finish it off.

Grouping shapes

When you have drawn a few shapes in a diagram, or other design, it can be a good thing to be able to move them around as a group. Shapes can be grouped easily by dragging across the shapes. This will select them all and Serif DrawPlus™ will offer to group them for you.

If you click on the Group button, the shapes are grouped and can be moved around as a single object.

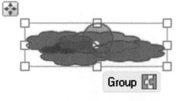

If you want to ungroup them, so that you can edit the group or just get at one of the shapes, you just select the group and click on the Ungroup button.

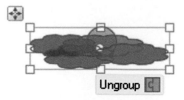

Gallery images

There are lots of images built into Serif DrawPlus™ that you can use in your designs.

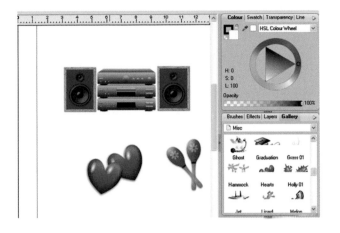

.Just click on the Gallery tab and have a look for what you need. You can also bring in other clip art and images from elsewhere.

Brushes

The Brush tool is very powerful.

You can still paint lines and use the spray can, but there are so many more choices at your fingertips!

The ordinary Brush tool can be tailored to whatever you want by using the Brush toolbar.

Brush: Line Colour   Width: 32 pt   Opacity: 100%   Flow: 100%

Here you can set the colour, thickness and transparency to suit your needs. You have almost as much flexibility as if you were using a set of real brushes! However you are not limited just to ordinary brushes. The galleries can let you stitch up your picture, or scatter diamonds over it. There are a range of galleries to explore. The drop down list allows you to choose from a wide variety of brush styles.

Try painting a few lines using a few styles.

Here is an example of the sort of thing that you can produce with the different brush galleries.

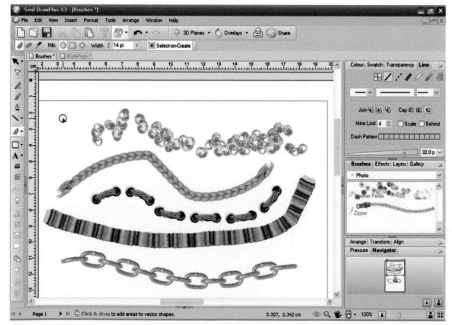

Project tasks

Use a digital photograph and the Brush tool to give the person a grunge, punk or rock makeover. Compare this image with those created by other members of your class. Discuss the visual impact of the changes you have chosen to apply.

Use the Stitches collection to create an advert for a fashion/design course. Compare your advert with those created by other members of your class. Discuss how you would adapt the advert to sell leather, denim or wool clothing. Try some of these new ideas out.

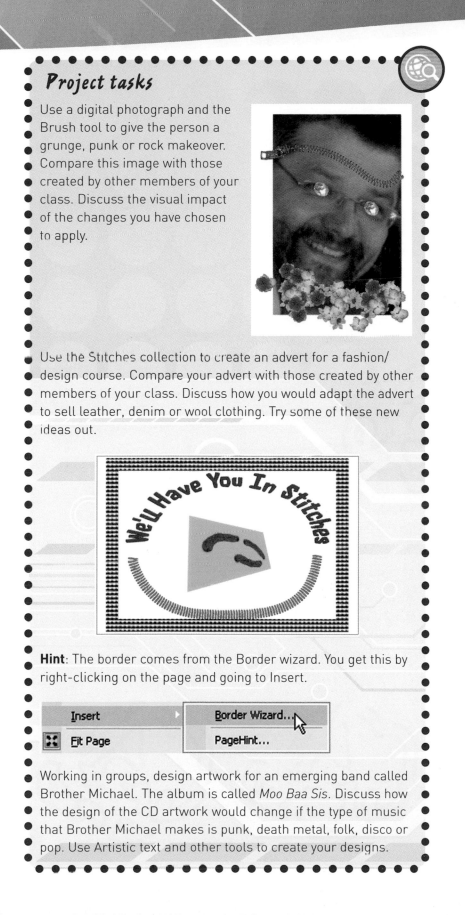

Hint: The border comes from the Border wizard. You get this by right-clicking on the page and going to Insert.

Working in groups, design artwork for an emerging band called Brother Michael. The album is called *Moo Baa Sis*. Discuss how the design of the CD artwork would change if the type of music that Brother Michael makes is punk, death metal, folk, disco or pop. Use Artistic text and other tools to create your designs.

Freeform paint

The Freeform paint tool allows us to apply many more effects.

These fall into three main categories: Paint, Erase and Knife.

Painting with the Freehand brush allows you to create this sort of flexible design.

We have chosen a yellow fill and a thick red outline (set at 5 pt) to create this racetrack.

Try this tool. Experimenting with the settings is the best way to learn.

The Eraser tool is rather self-explanatory! Just drag the Eraser tool over the selected object and those parts of the shape will be removed. Note that it is not just rubbing out bits of the shape and that the outlines will be reconnected.

The Knife tool is very powerful. Select the Knife and 'carve' a section from your shape. Clicking on part of the shape will remove that part. In the example below we have clicked on the slice and 'broken our heart'. If you shift-click on part of the shape then that will be the part retained instead.

Project tasks

Use a scanned or saved photo to create a graphic like the one shown here. You will need to use the Eraser to remove the unwanted edges and then the Knife tool to make the cut. Put gallery images inside the head and then move them forward/back until the layers look correct.

Use the Quick shapes and the Knife tool to create this design for a spider heart tattoo. You will need to slice all the way through and then use the Arrange toolbar to move the objects forward or back as shown on the left.

Use the Chinese calligraphy gallery to create a logo for a spa resort. The artistic text follows a circular path around the Chinese character for harmony.

Three-dimensional images

You can change any object in your design into a 3-D shape in a click!
Just draw a shape with any tool – we will use the flower Quick
shape.

Next click on the shape and click on the Instant 3-D button (it looks
like a little blue cube).

You should now have a 3-D flower!

Shocking shapes

Another effect that you can use to change an object is the Roughen
tool. This looks a bit like a small explosion.

Draw a shape to use for practice; we have used a red box with a
thick blue edge.

Select it and click on the Roughen tool. Drag your mouse across the
shape a few times to distort it.

Here we have done the same thing with a heart.

Applying effects to objects

You can use the Effects menu to add a special finish to any object in your design.

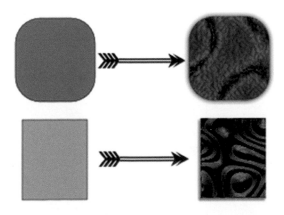

Just select the shape and go to the Effects palette. There are lots to choose from.

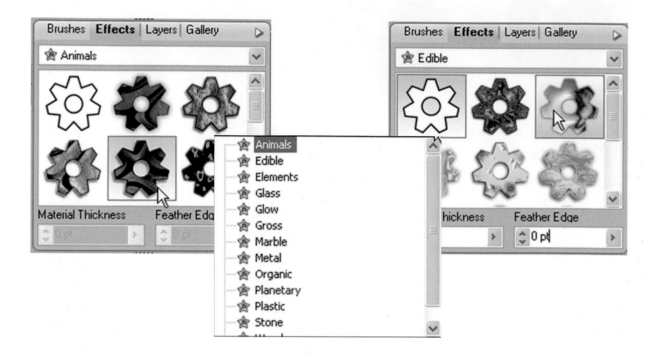

Try to create the following image using the effects of the same name from the Effects palette.

Project tasks

Use the tools you have been practising to create this sign for the snake house of a small zoo.

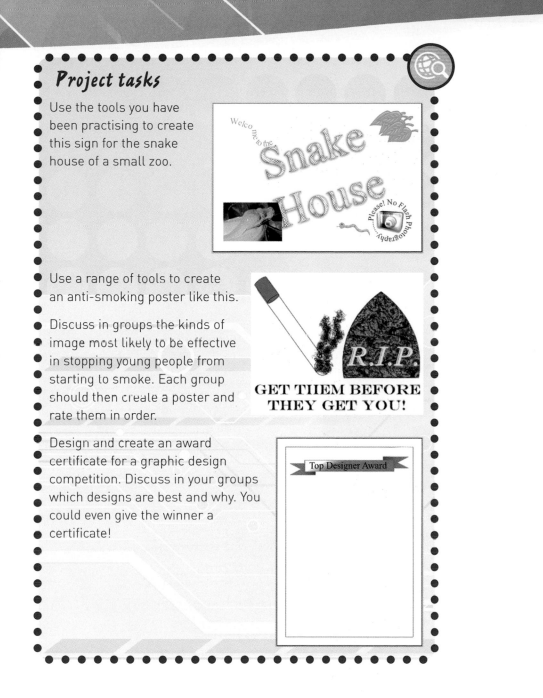

Use a range of tools to create an anti-smoking poster like this.

Discuss in groups the kinds of image most likely to be effective in stopping young people from starting to smoke. Each group should then create a poster and rate them in order.

Design and create an award certificate for a graphic design competition. Discuss in your groups which designs are best and why. You could even give the winner a certificate!

Removing the background from images

When working with images you might want to float a piece of clip art over your text. The cartoon skier here is a standard piece of clip art.

We are going to use the Cutout studio in Serif DrawPlus™ to turn it into the foreground character in a skiing postcard like the one below.

The stages are:

1 Choose your background image, your foreground character and any other shapes you want in the picture.

2 Choose a good image for your foreground figure. This should have a plain background, as it is easier for the software to remove all the unwanted sections of the image. The skier is very good because of the plain white background. However, the white background of the skier ruins our design, so we need to get rid of the background. For this we use the Cutout studio. Put the cartoon of the skier in a new drawing, click on it and select the Cutout studio button.

3 Use the Discard brush (the red eraser icon, second top on the left side of the window) to select the background colour by clicking and dragging some of the white area. This will select all the pixels of that colour. You can carefully select all the parts of the image that you want rid of before you hit OK.

4 This will leave you with a new image with a blue line around it. This should be pasted into your design. Now you can use what you have learnt to create your own postcard.

Remember: the best images to use for this type of design have white or plain backgrounds. It is very difficult to remove very 'busy' backgrounds with lots of details.

Project tasks

Use the Cutout studio to create a holiday postcard like the skiing example.

Use clip art or images from the Internet to design and create your own postcards. You could send a cartoon character to the pyramids or a dinosaur to the zoo!

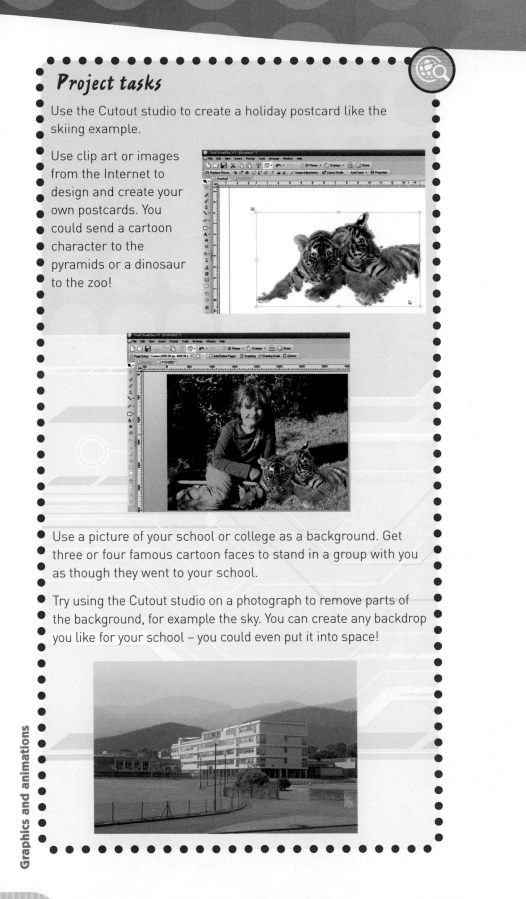

Use a picture of your school or college as a background. Get three or four famous cartoon faces to stand in a group with you as though they went to your school.

Try using the Cutout studio on a photograph to remove parts of the background, for example the sky. You can create any backdrop you like for your school – you could even put it into space!

Graphics and animations

Using Autotrace

The Autotrace feature in Serif DrawPlus™ allows you to add a range of effects to any image or photograph.

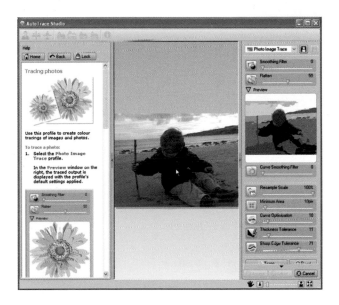

It also can convert a photograph into a group of objects. Below is the main screen of the Autotrace studio. It shows an image of a boy sitting on a beach.

By using the Autotrace facility and changing the positions of the sliders on the right of the screen, you can create a poster-like effect from the photograph.

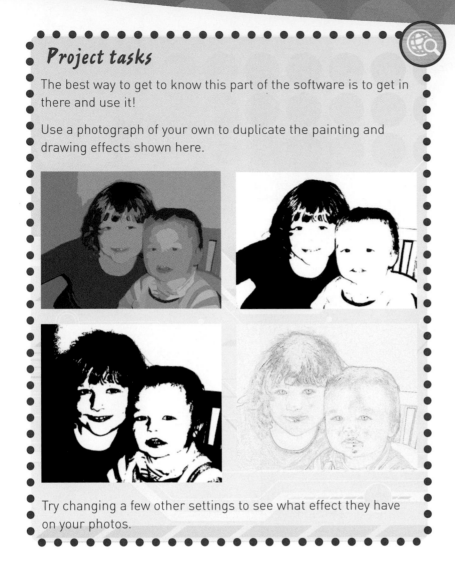

Animation

Animation uses a sequence of still images shown one after another quickly enough that the human brain is fooled into thinking that it is seeing a moving image. You can use Serif DrawPlus™ to create two types of animation. You can create either **Keyframe** or **Stopframe** animations.

Stopframe animation

Stopframe animation was explored in the Level 3 ICT book in the Pathways to Excellence series. This is the technique used in the film industry to produce films such as *the Curse of the Were-Rabbit* (from Nick Park and the fantastic team at Aardman) and stretches back into film history, with the likes of Ray Harryhausen's animated skeletons (have a look on the Internet!).

Here, small models are put into a miniature film set and a couple of pictures are taken. The model is moved slightly and another couple of pictures are taken. The whole process is repeated until you have a movie running at 24 frames per second. Each frame might have many characters making moves, so can take a while to set up. This means that you might only get a few seconds of film shot each day! Making stopframe movies can be a very long process and is very labour intensive. There is more material on stopframe on the Dynamic Learning website **www.dynamic-learning.co.uk** or in the Level 3 book.

Keyframe animation

We are going to look at keyframe animation in this book. The great thing about keyframe is that once you have set up your keyframes, the computer will do the rest of the work!

Keyframe animation uses a set of computer-generated objects. These are placed where you want them and given other attributes, such as rotation, and the whole image is stored as a frame (keyframe). The objects are then moved to a slightly different position in the frame and then stored again as a new keyframe. The computer will generate a number of steps between these two frames and this will give the illusion of smooth motion. This process is called Tweening.

Let's get started. First get a new file – a keyframe animation this time.

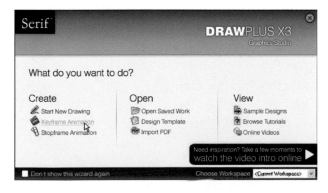

You will need to select the kind of keyframe animation that you want. Here we are going to choose a medium rectangle.

Next we import a background image into the animation.

Along the bottom of the screen is the Storyboard tab. This is a vital area, as it allows us to plan the sequence of keyframes. This is the order, running left to right, that the frames will play in when they are exported.

We will insert a number of frames into our animation and then add an object. Here we are using a small cartoon jet plane. By adding an object (such as the plane) to a starting keyframe you can have the software automatically copy this object forward onto the new frames as you create them. This process is called 'running forward' and it is the repositioning of these objects in later keyframes that gives the illusion of movement.

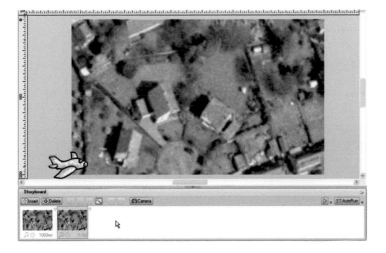

After we have added a few more frames, moving the plane along each time, we can see how the sequence is developing.

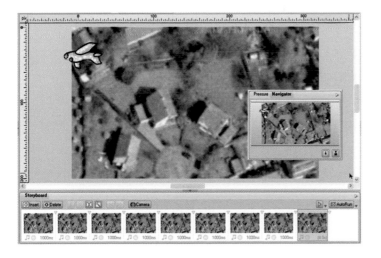

Notice the storyboard along the bottom. It shows that the whole clip is only eight seconds long.

You can preview your creation by clicking on the green arrow on the right of the storyboard.

This will create a Flash preview.

When you have completed your animation you will have to export it. This can be done in a range of formats. We are going to create a Flash animation (like you get on webpages) and a Quicktime movie.

Go to the File menu and choose 'Export' and then select 'Export as Flash SWF'. The SWF stands for Shockwave Flash.

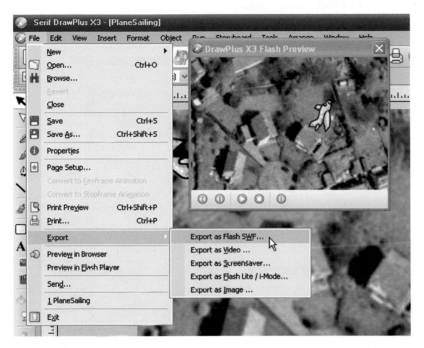

Choose where you want to save the file and what you want it to be called.

Now play it to test it out.

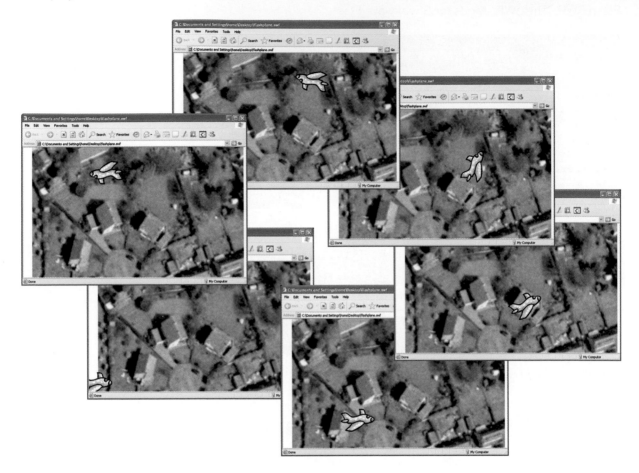

The process is just the same for creating a Quicktime movie. Just pick the settings that you want and export the movie!

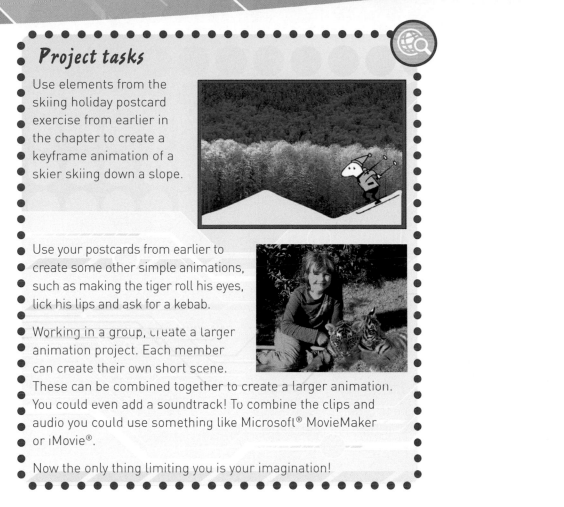

Project tasks

Use elements from the skiing holiday postcard exercise from earlier in the chapter to create a keyframe animation of a skier skiing down a slope.

Use your postcards from earlier to create some other simple animations, such as making the tiger roll his eyes, lick his lips and ask for a kebab.

Working in a group, create a larger animation project. Each member can create their own short scene. These can be combined together to create a larger animation. You could even add a soundtrack! To combine the clips and audio you could use something like Microsoft® MovieMaker or iMovie®.

Now the only thing limiting you is your imagination!

Assessment

Self-assessment

Make sure you have completed all your individual checklists and questionnaires and a group questionnaire for each project. These are available in the Appendix at the back of the book.

Teacher assessment

Your teacher will ask you to place the working files you used to store the information you collected from magazines and the Internet for each project in your portfolio.

If your teacher has access to the dynamic learning materials, you will be asked to complete some online quizzes.

Your teacher will also assess the group's wiki or e-group when you have completed each project as well as how well you have worked as a group.

6

Linking up

We are going to look at a few resources and ways of working that you can use to collaborate with other people, structure what you already know and link to new knowledge. We are going to look at:

- email
- texting
- blogging
- podcasts
- social networking sites
- social changes.

Email

One of the easiest ways to pass around information is by using **email**. You will probably have your own private email at home. You will have been issued with an email address at your school or college. You even have an email address on Glow!

Your school or Glow email addresses are not the same as your private email. Staff at your school or college will have access to these as they are supposed to be for educational purposes and they are legally responsible for monitoring the use (and sometimes abuse) of their email system. You should check with your school to see the details of what is covered by their policies.

Your private email will either come with your Internet access contract or be web based. For the first of these, your Internet service provider (ISP) will have given one or more email addresses for use by the contract holder. They will look something like this:

johnmason@tiscali.co.uk

john.mason@btinternet.co.uk

masonjohn@sky.co.uk

The other way to get an email address is to go to any web-based email provider and sign up! There are many different providers such as Google Inc.'s Gmail™, Microsoft® Hotmail® or Yahoo!®. All of these will offer similar services and it is a matter of personal preference which one you use.

Any email system needs to be able to identify you uniquely from all the other users. Sometimes it can be quite difficult to think up a name – particularly if you have quite a common name to start with! Most email providers will offer you a few suggestions when you find that the cool name you were going to use is already taken.

The other thing that you have to come up with is a password. This should not be easy to guess, as it is what stands between you and someone who might want to pretend to be you online.

Password strength increases if you make your password longer. You should include two or three of the following:

- Upper case letters – A, B, C etc.
- Lower case letters – a, b, c, etc.
- Numbers – 0, 1, 2 etc.
- Punctuation – dash, full stop, comma etc.

Your password needs to be easy to remember, but not easy to guess. Some techniques are:

- Use numbers inside words instead of letters – Snai1mai1.
- Combine words to make nonsense words – cat + dog = Cdaotg.
- Create a memorable image – Arr0w=>.

Common useful features of email are:

- **Email groups**: A number of emails can be grouped together under one name. this means that you can set up a group of your close friends, a sports team, your ICT class or your family. This means that you can send one email and all the members of the group will get it.
- **Attachments**: A file, or files, can be attached to an email and sent with it. This means that you can send homework in to school, photos to friends or even chapters of a book to a publisher! Most email providers limit the size of your email attachments, so that the system does not grind to a halt.
- **Folders/directories**: These allow you to store old emails in relevant groups/folders so that they don't just clutter up your inbox and you can find what you are looking for more easily.

Common problems of email are:

- **Junk email**: A lot of the emails that are received on a daily basis, particularly if you do a lot of web surfing, are junk mail. This is unsolicited, and unwanted, email that is sent to you automatically by companies that think you might buy some of their products. Much of the junk mail is about buying cheap medicines over the Internet (a dodgy practice in terms of legality and personal safety!) or about selling you pornography of one type or another. The email lists that these companies hold are passed around to other companies, often owned by the same people, and the computer will send out emails to thousands (or even millions) of people every day. It is a very cheap way for the companies to seek out new business, but it is very annoying to find your inbox clogged up with them. Junk mail is also called 'spam' (just do a search for Monty Python Vikings if you want to know why it is called spam). Don't open junk and never reply to it, it will only get worse. You should report spam to your email provider if they have that option available.
- **Chain email**: This can be quite cruel in the way they try to bully you into sending them on. You read the email and then send it on to 10 friends, so that they can pass it on in turn. In just a few days this email can be sitting in millions of inboxes. These can sometimes be used to gather email addresses to sell on to the junk email companies.
- **Viruses, worms and trojans**: A computer **virus** is a malicious file, or files, that can be attached to an email and arrive on your computer when you view the email. A virus is a small program that copies itself and spreads between computers – just like a flu virus spreads between humans. Viruses can be attached to

emails or any other file and can be set to run the minute you open the host file. A **worm** is like a virus, but it does not need a host. It is like a parasite, it copies itself across networks, always looking for another computer to jump to. They can move quite fast across networks and are often quite destructive. A **trojan** is a malicious program that appears to be something else, like a game. When you download and play the game the trojan will be doing something else behind your back! These programs are all types of **malware**. Get a good anti-virus program installed and keep it up to date. You could pay for something like Norton or McAfee, or just download a free one like 'AVG free'. For more on this subject see Unit 3.

Email allows you to work or communicate with people right across the world. Email is often a jump off point for many other web-based methods of information sharing.

Project tasks

Find out the details of the email use policy in your school. Discuss in groups whether you think each of the rules is fair and reasonable. Discuss why each of these rules is in the policy? Are there any other rules that should be in the policy? If you come up with a better set of rules perhaps you could submit them to the senior management of your school/college and maybe get the policy updated!

Create a poster/leaflet of these rules that you can put up in your ICT room.

Working in groups, discuss a number of different email providers. Compare different features. How are they the same? How do they differ?

Working with others, find out what the maximum size of files that can be attached to an email in as many email providers as you can.

Create a leaflet/poster setting out some guidelines of good practice for email use. You could include rules of 'netiquette' (good manners/behaviour online), advice on the maximum size of attachments and the fact that all emails should have a clear subject line with a statement of what the email is about.

Use the Internet to make a list of common viruses and worms. List their names, the date they first appeared and the sort of damage that they cause.

Texting

Texting is everywhere. Almost everyone in the UK has a mobile phone. Each text, or SMS, is around 160 characters or less and can be sent to one or more person wherever they are in the world. Like email, the text will sit on the mobile phone company server until the person you are sending to switches their phone on.

Each number key can stand for a letter, for example, the number 2 can be 'a', 'b' or 'c'.

You might send texts that use full English words and punctuation, such as:

> 'Send a text to a friend, it will help you stay in touch about something you are doing later.'

Or, more probably, it might look something like this:

> 'Snd a txt 2 a m8 it will help u stay in touch about wot u r doing l8r'

The second version allows you to send much more information in the same number of characters. Basically, this encoding of data is what computers are all about! Some people are quite worried, or just plain grumpy, about the effect of 'text-speak' on the English language, but language will always change to reflect those using it and those changes are usually resisted by the generation before.

One smart feature of phones is **predictive text**. This is the feature that allows the program in the phone to 'guess' what word it is that you mean without having to type the whole thing out. It works by comparing the keys you are pressing against the list of words it knows and coming up with the word that is most likely to be correct.

Sometimes it will make a mistake and give you a different word. This is because it has the same pattern of keys and is more commonly used. Each time you use a word the program adds one to its score. So you can change the order of words in the list by using 'of' more often than 'me'. These are both '63' and you will be offered 'of' as the default option first and have to change it to 'me'. If you do that often enough during texting, the order of these words in the list will switch and the phone will start suggesting 'me' instead of 'of'.

Examples of texting 'siblings':

Keys pressed	List of possible words in order of score
4663	good, home, gone, hood
5646	John, join, logo, IMHO, loin
43	he, if
63	of, me

Project tasks

Copy the above table, adding a few more rows of your own 'siblings'.

Use the words to show how mistakes can be made in texting, for example texting 'He is gone' rather than 'He is home' sends quite the opposite message. Working in groups, discuss how a lack of care when texting can lead to misunderstandings.

Many smart phones have full 'qwerty' keyboards. In groups, discuss how this has changed texting.

Some phones have touchscreens instead of actual keys. In your groups, discuss the advantages and disadvantages of each of these methods. You might want to consider things like alternative alphabets on touchscreens.

Blogging

A blog is just like an online diary. The name comes from 'web log'. You can find a blog on almost any topic you can imagine. You may have a blog as part of your Facebook® page, so that you can let your friends know what you are up to. You might subscribe to a blog on a particular topic that interests you.

One other way of getting out into the world of blogging is through Twitter.

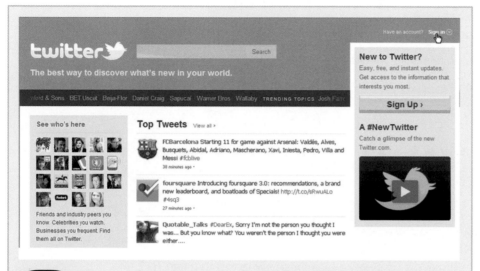

Twitter is a kind of social networking and blogging site. It has been around since 2006 and is very popular, with a huge number of subscribers on a huge number of topics.

Twitter is used for 'microblogging'. You are limited to only 140 characters in each of your posts, or 'Tweets'. Users, or 'Tweeters', can type their comments into the website or post them by phone via SMS from anywhere in the world to their page on the site.

Any other user can read these tweets, as all tweets are publicly visible until the user sets up restrictions. You can restrict your Tweets to a list of your 'followers'. These are people who have chosen to receive your comments directly. In 2011 there were nearly 200 million members posting over 65 million Tweets on Twitter every day!

Project tasks

Use your school email system to emulate a site like Twitter. The easiest way is to create a group in your own email called 'followers' and add several people to it. Your microblogs can now be sent to the group and it will work just like Twitter.

After you have tried this experiment for a few days, have a look at the sort of things being blogged. Divide the messages into categories and count up the proportion of messages that are related to work, chat, humour, etc. Discuss this as a group. Use the Internet to find out about research carried out on actual Twitter traffic. How does this compare with what you found? You could create a presentation or poster of your findings.

Try out your literacy skills! Can you write a haiku (a short Japanese poem) in 140 characters? How about a limerick? ('There was a young man from Fife, who wanted the most out of life...')

Get together with others to write a short play. Several of you could act the parts and 'Tweet' your lines.

Twitter / Home - Internet Explorer provided by Dell

http://twitter.com/#

Norton · | Norton Safe Search | Search | ✓ Safe Web · | 🔒 Identity Safe ·

☆ Favorites | 🖼 🏉 Suggested Sites · | 🏉 Web Slice Gallery ·

🔠 · | M Gmail - Confirm your Twit... | 🐦 Twitter / Home | × | 🌃 Welcome to Facebook — ...

twitter | Search | 🔍 | Home Profile Messa

What's happening?

Timeline @Mentions Retweets ▾ Searches ▾ Lists ▾

What's happening? | ×

Hi twitterers! Here I am typing stuff, trying to meet a deadline, and Michael, my two year old son, has just got up. Work stops life starts.

0 | Tweet

Podcasts

One fast growing area of the web is that of the 'podsphere'. A podcast is just like a broadcast, but it is a downloadable file that you can carry with you and play where and when you like. The podcast could be either video or audio, and sometimes you even get the choice. There are literally millions of podcasts on thousands of topics. The Apple iTunes® Store has a whole section where you can get podcasts, many for free!

Or a quick Internet search can get you podcasts on a range of topics, serious or otherwise.

http://LibriVox.org is well worth a visit, or perhaps you could find something to help you learn the periodic table on YouTube! There is always the BBC website, a rich source of quality podcasts.

Making a podcast could not be easier. All you need is some sound editing software. You might have some bundled with your computer (like GarageBand® from Apple) or just download something like Audacity® (**http://www.download-audacity.com**). This is a great little program and it's free!

Audacity® lets you edit the sounds that you capture with the microphone on your computer and then save them as an mp3 file. Then you just need to upload them and you are off!

Try to find out if your school or college is involved with the Radiowaves project (**http://www.radiowaves.co.uk**), as this might be a good way of distributing your work.

It is very important to remember that if you use other people's material in your podcast and then put it on the web, through YouTube or similar, you will need to ask permission from the owners of that material. Using the work of others, whether you get paid or not, is a breach of copyright and could get you into serious trouble.

Project tasks

Working on your own or in a group, write a short script for a podcast of a news bulletin. This could be a local news story, or even something from your school or college. It should be around 30 seconds long.

In larger groups, combine the individual news stories into a three-minute radio broadcast. You could have news, sport, weather and then that humorous story about the skateboarding squirrel at the end.

Working on your own or in a group, create a podcast of a short story, poem or short scene from a play.

Working on your own or in a group, create a podcast to help others learn a topic at school or college. Share these with others, perhaps using the school network or Radiowaves.

Search the Internet for a good example of a podcast of *each* of the following types. Share your list with others in your class.

- Music from an unsigned band
- An audiobook
- A historical lecture/lesson
- Learning another language
- Stand-up comedy
- Science/Technology
- Medical news
- News reporting.

Social networking sites

This is a very common method of having a 'presence' online. There are literally hundreds of different social networking websites.

Social networking is not a new thing. The Internet itself could be said to have been an early social network. ARPANET allowed scientists to share ideas and communicate over distance more easily and this was soon extended as other networks linked in and the Internet was born! Early communication was a bit like a clunky version of Twitter or 'bit torrent' sites, with short messages or just lists of files for download that you were unsure of until you actually opened them!

Soon there were loads of options, as user groups for specific areas of study/interest sprang up. The real change came when Tim Berners-Lee dreamt up the idea of pages containing text and graphics that could be viewed and shared live across the Internet. And so, the Web was born! Sites like Friendster℠ allowed you to manage lists of friends and share information through a home page. MySpace and Bebo became popular over this period. Then, in 2004, Facebook® arrived!

Facebook® was created by Mark Zuckerberg and friends so that students of Harvard University could exchange messages and other information. This was slowly expanded to students and pupils of other universities and schools. Now anyone can have a page on Facebook® just by signing up and claiming to be at least 13 years old. There are more than 600 million active inhabitants of the Facebook® world!

There are plenty of other alternatives to the Facebook® site.

Many people start off as 'e-citizens' in other worlds, such as Habbo® Hotel or Disney's Club Penguin, before moving to the more 'grown-up' sites. This lets young people learn how to keep themselves safe online before stepping onto the wider stage of the Internet.

There are loads of more specialised social networking sites. These are often aimed at particular groups with something in common, such as a particular sport or hobby. The site might have a religious focus, such as the Muslim site **http://muxlim.com**.

One of the early social networking sites was MySpace. This has been in a bit of a decline more recently, but still plays host to a thriving musical community. Many bands, record labels and emerging artists use MySpace as their main Internet presence. In other parts of the world, such as South America, it is Google Inc.'s networking site Orkut™ that is the dominant player.

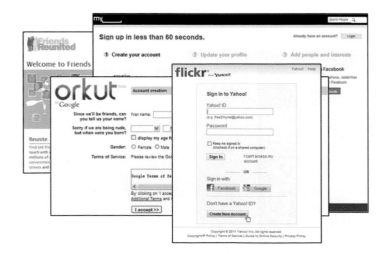

Whatever site you use, you need to make sure you know who has access to your information.

The default setting for Facebook® is to have *everything* visible for *everyone*. This can make it easier if you want your stuff to be *really* open, but most only want friends and family to have full access.

Make sure that you check how to change your profile and how you share your photos and other data.

Project tasks

Discuss in your groups which social networking sites the class use. Try to make a list of the common features that they have and other features that make each one stand out from the crowd.

Discuss how many online 'friends' you each have and what you mean by a 'friend'. How has the concept of 'friend' been changed by our use of social networking sites?

Discuss some of these other questions in your groups:

- How many of you lied about personal details when you set up your page?
- What sorts of 'lies' are 'acceptable' when building an online presence?
- How many of your online friends are not exactly as they appear on screen?
- Just how secure is your online data? How many others have access to it?

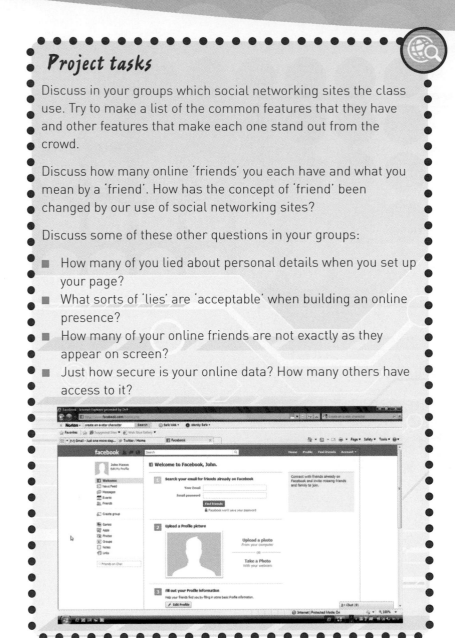

Social changes

Discussion topic 1

Social networks are changing the way that we live. We can update our Facebook® page from our smartphone as we move through our life. If we choose to, we can let our friends know where we are and what we are doing every second of our day.

Project task

Divide into groups. Each group should pick one of the discussion topics below. Discuss the issue in your group and create a presentation to share the debate with the rest of the class.

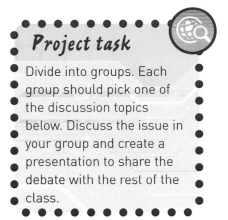

Discussion topic 2

This is a table showing those networking sites and other online, or virtual, communities with more than a hundred million active users in early 2011.

Site name	Number of active user accounts in millions
Twitter	190
Facebook®	600
Gmail™	185
Orkut™	120
Habbo®	203

Discussion topic 3

President Obama was praised for his use of the Internet during the campaign that got him elected as the President of the United States. He raised a lot of money by contacting his supporters through sites like Facebook®.

Discussion topic 4

Many charities and other organisations now have Facebook® pages as well as ordinary webpages. Through these sites they have access to millions of potential supporters every day.

Discussion topic 5

As the power of hardware improves and we use these devices more they will become an essential part of our lives. In July 2010, Finland made it a legal right that every citizen should have broadband access (at 1 Mbps) to the Internet. This will be improved to 100 Mbps by 2015.

guardian.co.uk

News | Sport | Comment | Culture | Business | Money | Life & style | Travel | Environment | T

News ⟩ Technology ⟩ Broadband

Finland makes broadband access a legal right

Bobbie Johnson, technology correspondent
guardian.co.uk, Wednesday 14 October 2009 18.40 BST
Article history

A larger | smaller

Technology
Broadband · Internet · Telecoms

Business
Telecommunications industry

World news
Finland

More news

See also
14 Aug 2011
Superfast broadband gets ready to go UK-wide
6 Jun 2008
Code agreed on broadband ads
10 Feb 2010
Google to test ultra fast broadband lines
4 Mar 2009
Path cleared for BT's superfast broadband

The Finnish government has become the first in the world to make broadband internet access a legal right.

According to local reports, the Ministry of Transport and Communications in Helsinki has pushed through a law that will force telecommunications providers to offer high speed internet connections to all of the country's 5.3 million citizens.

Discussion topic 6

In 2011, it was reported that every iPhone® was using satellite navigation to record the movements of its user on a regular basis. There seemed to be no justification for this data gathering and it was just lying in a folder on the iPhone® unused.

Discussion topic 7

In May 2010, a couple from South Korea were arrested after their three-month-old baby, Anime, starved to death. They were addicted to online gaming and would go out to all-night Internet cafés to play online. They were raising a fantasy child in their online world, but neglected their real child.

Assessment

Self-assessment

Make sure you have completed all your individual checklists and questionnaires and a group questionnaire for each project. These are available in the Appendix at the back of the book.

Teacher assessment

Your teacher will ask you to place the working files you used to store the information you collected from magazines and the Internet for each project in your portfolio.

If your teacher has access to the dynamic learning materials, you will be asked to complete some online quizzes.

Your teacher will also assess the group's wiki or e-group when you have completed each project as well as how well you have worked as a group.

Answers

1 Researching computer technologies

Progress check! Page 16

graphics card	This processes the images on your computer, freeing up the main processor so that it can get on with other tasks.
systems analyst	This person's task is to decide what hardware and software is needed.
resolution	This is used to describe the quality of an image on a screen, e.g. 1280 x 1024.
browser	This is a program that helps you navigate the World Wide Web by moving between and looking at web pages.
server	This is a powerful computer with a fast processor and large memory capacity which provides the resources on a network, e.g. file storage.
sound card	This processes the sounds on your computer, freeing up the main processor so that it can get on with other tasks.
processor	The 'brain' of the computer that deals with all the movement of data and any calculations to be carried out.
RAM	This part of the memory holds all of the programs and data files currently in use by the system and the user.
simulation	This uses computer-based models to train people and to help them develop skills, such as driving a car or flying a plane.
Gigabyte	This is used to measure the size of memory and hard drive capacity.
GHz	This is used to measure the clock speed of a processor.
virtual reality	This is an advanced form of simulation that can create the illusion that the user is part of the computer's world.

Key points task Page 19

Key points:

- 'it can be difficult to read words on an LCD display'
- 'the Kindle's electronic ink screen looks more like paper than an LCD screen'
- 'it reflects light in much the same way that paper does'
- 'you'll need daylight or an external light source to read anything'
- 'Amazon Kindle 2 can hold up to 1,500 titles'
- 'with a Kindle, you don't have to worry about packing heavy books in your luggage to last for the whole trip'
- 'you can always use the Kindle to access Amazon's store and buy a new book'.

Combining Key Points:

Reading from an LCD screen can be difficult. A Kindle's screen is more like ordinary paper and you need daylight or a lamp in order to read it. A Kindle can hold thousands of titles and saves you from carrying lots of books about with you. You can even download books onto your Kindle from Amazon.

Key points task Page 20

Key points:

- customers don't own their main computers
- they rent access to them and pay a monthly bill
- this makes better use of expensive equipment and servers
- this lowers costs and lets customers use a wide range of software.

Combining Key Points:

In cloud computing customers don't own their computers but have shared access to them and pay a monthly rental bill. Sharing computers in this way lowers costs and lets them use a wide range of software.

2 Computing technology, the economy and the environment

Progress check! Page 26

There could be an endless list for this task, including schools, hospitals, doctors surgeries, factories, libraries, offices, police stations, supermarkets, airports, travel agents, railway companies, car manufacturers, etc.

Progress check! Page 27

50 watts x 24 kilowatt hours
= 1200 watt hours per day
= 1.2 kilowatt hours per day.

In one year that = 365 x 1.2 kilowatt hours
= 438 kilowatt hours.

At 10p per kilowatt hour the cost = £43.80

3 Which security suite?

Progress check! Page 44

Match the following using the terms given below.

Designed to track and monitor user keystrokes, often used to steal passwords and credit card numbers.	*Keylogger*
False security software that tries to frighten the user into buying it.	*Scareware*
A remote access trojan which gives control of your computer to a hacker.	*RAT*
A program that makes copies of itself and then spreads through a network, damaging systems as it goes along.	*worm*
A program that makes copies of itself, attaches itself to programs you have installed on your computer and then damages your system.	*virus*
Your system crashes after you have downloaded files from a P2P website.	*P2P infection*

Progress check! Page 44

Name the type of malware at work when:

1 Adverts are constantly appearing on your computer. *Adware*

2 You install a piece of software because it claims to make your computer work faster, but all sorts of funny things start to happen. *Trojan*

3 Your browser has a design weakness. *Browser exploit*

4 A business sends you an email stating that you have won £1,000,000. All you have to do is send your bank account details and they will pay it into your account. *Phishing*

5 A piece of software is installed which lets other people control your computer. *Rootkit*

Research task Page 45

Now list the features that the free package does not have.

The free package does not have online shield (P2P) protection, advanced rootkit protection, gaming mode protection, phishing protection, identity protection and anti-spam.

Explain why you would get better protection using one of the payment packages.

These features would give added protection from threats that might get through if you were using the free version.

Research task Page 46

The report could choose the Defender suite because it gives lots more protection than the Panther suite and it stopped more malware in the tests that were run. It could be rejected because it lacks automatic updates.

The Panther suite could be chosen because it is easy to install, run and update, but it could be rejected because it gives less protection against threats and stopped less malware in the tests.

Research task Page 47

The Alert suite defends against the least number of threats and performed the worst in tests. It is therefore the easiest to reject even though it is free.

The Walls suite could be chosen because it defends against more threats than the Alert suite and it updates automatically, but it could be rejected because it only stopped 80 per cent of malware on tests and, at £42, is the most expensive suite.

The Police suite could be chosen because it defends against the greatest number of threats and stops the most malware in tests. Also it only costs £30. It could be rejected because it lacks automatic updates, is not as easy as the others to use and also charges for support.

Appendix

Self-assessment

Now that you have completed this section it's time to check how you got on.

If you created some web pages then complete this simple questionnaire and then discuss it with your teacher and/or the others in your group.

Name ....

Project ....

Did I plan carefully?	
Did I choose a suitable colour for my home page?	
Does my home page contain clear links to all my other pages?	
Is the information on each of my pages relevant to the topic?	
Can you read the text on my pages easily?	
Do the graphics on my pages fit the text and add to the meaning?	
Are there any useful links to Internet sites on my pages?	
Do I have any useful sound files or video clips on my pages?	
Is there anything I should have added to my website to improve it?	
Any other comments on my website.	

Self-assessment

Now that you have completed this section it's time to check how you got on.

If you created some web pages then complete this simple questionnaire and then discuss it with your teacher and/or the others in your group.

Group ....

Project ....

Did our group plan together?	
Did everyone join in the discussions?	
Did we choose a suitable colour for our home page?	
Does our home page contain clear links to all our other pages?	
Is the information on each of our pages relevant to the topic?	
Can you read the text on our pages easily?	
Do the graphics on our pages fit the text and add to the meaning?	
Are there any useful links to Internet sites on our pages?	
Do we have any useful sound files or video clips on our pages?	
Is there anything we should have added to our website to improve it?	
Did each member of the group have a clear task?	
Did each member of the group complete their task?	
What were the key things we learnt when completing our project?	
Any other comments on our website.	

Self-assessment

Now that you have completed this section it's time to check how you got on.

If you created some presentations then complete this simple questionnaire and then discuss it with your teacher and/or the others in your group.

Name ....

Project ....

Did I plan carefully?	
Did I choose a suitable layout for my slides?	
Is the information on each of my slides relevant to the topic?	
Can you read the text on my slides easily?	
Are the slide colour and text colours suitable?	
Do the graphics on my slides fit the text and add to the meaning?	
Are there any useful links to Internet sites on my slides?	
Do I have any useful sound files or video clips on my slides?	
Is there anything I should have added to my presentation to improve it?	
What were the key things I learnt when completing my presentation?	
Any other comments on my presentation.	

Self-assessment

Now that you have completed this section it's time to check how you got on.

If you created some presentations then complete this simple questionnaire and then discuss it with your teacher and/or the others in your group.

Group ....

Project ....

Did our group plan together?	
Did everyone join in the discussions?	
Did we choose a suitable colour for the slides and for the text?	
Is the information on each of our slides relevant to the topic?	
Can you read the text on our slides easily?	
Do the graphics on our slides fit the text and add to the meaning?	
Are there any useful links to Internet sites on our slides?	
Do we have any useful sound files or video clips on our slides?	
Is there anything we should have added to our presentation to improve it?	
Did each member of the group have a clear task?	
Did each member of the group complete their task?	
What were the key things we learnt when completing our project?	
Any other comments on our presentation.	

Self-assessment

Now that you have completed this section it's time to check how you got on.

If you created some posters then complete this simple questionnaire and then discuss it with your teacher and/or the others in your group.

Name ....

Project ....

Did I plan carefully?	
Did I choose a suitable layout for my posters?	
Is the information on each of my posters relevant to the topic?	
Can you read the text on my posters easily?	
Are the background colours and text colours suitable?	
Do the graphics on my posters fit the text and add to the meaning?	
Are there any useful pointers to Internet sites on my posters?	
Is there anything I should have added to my posters to improve them?	
What were the key things I learnt when completing my posters?	
Any other comments on my set of posters.	

Self-assessment

Now that you have completed this section it's time to check how you got on.

If you created some posters then complete this simple questionnaire and then discuss it with your teacher and/or the others in your group.

Group ....

Project ....

Did our group plan together?	
Did everyone join in the discussions?	
Did we choose a suitable colour for the background and for the text?	
Is the information on each of our posters relevant to the topic?	
Can you read the text on our posters easily?	
Do the graphics on our posters fit the text and add to the meaning?	
Are there any useful pointers to Internet sites on our posters?	
Do we have any useful sound files or video clips on our posters?	
Is there anything we should have added to our posters to improve them?	
Did each member of the group have a clear task?	
Did each member of the group complete their task?	
What were the key things we learnt when completing our posters?	
Any other comments on our set of posters.	

Self-assessment

Now that you have completed this section it's time to check how you got on.

If you created a wiki then complete this simple questionnaire and then discuss it with your teacher and/or the others in your group.

Group ....

Project ....

Did our group plan together?	
Did everyone join in the discussions?	
Does our home page contain clear links to all our other pages?	
Is the information on each of our pages relevant to the topic?	
Can you read the text on our pages easily?	
Do the graphics on our pages fit the text and add to the meaning?	
Are there any useful links to Internet sites on our pages?	
Is there anything we should have added to our website to improve it?	
Did each member of the group have a clear task?	
Did each member of the group complete their task?	
What were the key things we learnt when completing our project?	
Any other comments on our website.	

Group project planning sheet

Group ....

Project ....

Sources of information	
Recording information	
Group communication	
How our information will be presented	
Time plan with target deadlines	

Assessing my contribution to the group's task

Name ....

How well did I contribute to the discussion for the planning and the comparison?	
How well did I listen to other people when discussing ideas?	
How well did I use the Internet/magazine articles to find useful information?	
How well did I keep to the deadlines the group set out?	
How well did I produce clear wiki/web pages or presentation slides with useful information and graphics?	
Did I help other people with their tasks?	

Assessing our group work: Comparing low power PCs

Assessing our group work: Comparing low power PCs	
How well did we listen to each other's ideas when discussing the planning and the comparison?	
How well did we manage any disagreements?	
Did we keep on track and meet our deadlines or did we fall behind?	
Did the group find enough good information and select the key points?	
Did we share the data with the group using email or a wiki?	
Was the final version of our wiki/website/ presentation clear and easy to understand?	
Was the final version of our wiki/website/ presentation attractive?	
Was the final version of our wiki/website/ presentation easy to use with plenty of information?	

Security suite project

Name ....

Assessment checklist	Date Completed
Completed the planning sheet	
Completed the research	
Recorded the key points of information	
Emailed the information files	
Completed our wiki pages	
Discussed the security suite comparison and entered it on the wiki	
Completed the assessment sheets	
Presented the wiki to the class and teacher	

Assessing our group work: Security suite research task

How well did we listen to each other's ideas when discussing the planning and the comparison?	
How well did we manage any disagreements?	
Did we keep on track and meet our deadlines or did we fall behind?	
Did the group find enough good information and select the key points?	
Did we share the data with the group using email and the wiki?	
Was the final version of our wiki clear and easy to understand?	
Was the final version of our wiki attractive?	
Was the final version of our wiki easy to use with plenty of links between the pages?	